Everyday Comfort

100 of your favourite comfort
foods reimagined with nourishing
twists and healthy hacks

Katie Pix

@thekatiepix

Photography by
Izy Hossack

quadrille

Introduction

My grandma's leek and potato soup is unmatchable. There's no big secret to it; just take a King Edward and the dirtiest leek you can find, cook it down with some gloriously savoury, salty chicken stock and add a terrifying amount of cream. With one mouthful I'm transported, sitting in a pebble-dashed townhouse in Liverpool, taking the skin off the roof of my mouth with this piping hot elixir while excitedly awaiting the fireworks to start on the first Bonfire Night I can remember.

The dishes that have a hold on our hearts are about so much more than sustenance and fuel – they're like little bookmarks slotted between the pages of our lives. They lie there quietly, until one day, roaming the streets of Paris, WHAM, it hits you: that sourdough scent tickling your nostrils, and (if you're me) your mind wanders to Christmas '99 when Dad, at the last second, decided against the over-large roller skates and instead opted for a bread-maker for Mum. She fired it up immediately on a freezing Christmas morning and gave us the best smoked salmon and scrambled egg breakfast ever.

For me, that's what comfort food is all about – the dishes that connect us to the moments we felt happiest and safest, edible time-machines that strip away the stresses of the day-to-day and just make us really, really content.

Irritatingly, however, a lot of these foods are an indulgence, filled with yummy fats, sugars and, likely, cheese. Sure, they're pretty irresistible, but we tend to save them for a necessary occasion: a rainy day, a heartbreak, a time of uncertainty and self-doubt. We treat them as 'break glass in case of emergency' cooking, not something for the day-to-day.

Until you bought this book, that is.

This book transforms a whole host of my comfort classics into accessible, balanced, repeatable, and (most importantly) insanely delicious reincarnations that will leave you satisfied in soul, stomach and mind, and can be eaten every day. Packed with quick hacks and cool twists that create new memories with your old favourites, this is your incomparable kitchen companion when you just need that comforting hit, but don't want to binge yourself on a whole block of Cheddar.

Each chapter of this book is based on a classic comfort-food category, from Friday-night takeaways to your Sunday roast, and everything in between. So whatever you've got a hankering for, you know exactly where to turn to scratch that itch in double quick time.

And for those moments when you need something super-duper quick, sprinkled throughout the book are a selection of deliciously snacky pick-me-ups – guaranteed to become immediate favourites you'll knock up again and again whenever the urge takes you.

Great food can turn even the most rubbish day into a great one – and this book is all about giving you the kitchen superpower of making every day an absolute belter – and know you're doing your body as much good as your soul.

A LITTLE ABOUT ME

A little about me

It's 2009. I'm just starting my first week at university and, as I watch my mum and dad's car leaving campus, my stomach begins churning with fear and early-onset homesickness. I realize – far too late – that I am NOT ready for this.

Freshers' Week is apparently a blur of Pot Noodles, wild parties, and even wilder hangovers. Nope. Not for me. Mine was spent tearfully erecting a shrine to my home town, punctuated by panic-stricken calls to my mum and dad. Words of wisdom from my anchors? Sort of. What I wanted was Dad's beef stroganoff recipe and Mum's spaghetti bolognese.

It was at university that I found my passion for food. But I wasn't searching for new flavours and textures; I was frantically trying to bring a little piece of home into my dingy dorm room.

Food has always been at the centre of my world. Both of my parents are chefs, and Mum and Dad would bring my brother and me into the kitchen from a really young age, talking us through the processes that turned raw ingredients into gorgeous food. Their classical training meant that sauces and bases were high on this home-baked curriculum, so the first recipe I ever properly learned was a bechamel sauce... to which I immediately started adding terrifying amounts of cheese, as my cooking displays a strong tendency towards gluttony.

After graduation, I was desperate to find a job that blended my love of food with my passion for social media, and after a few years specializing in PR relations for several British food brands, I was offered the chance to tweet, post and Instagram for Mr Jamie Oliver.

I was over the moon. Jamie's was the first cookery show I'd ever watched, the first recipe book I'd ever owned and the first person I'd ever aspired to be. He has this supernatural understanding of what people like to eat, and he also happens to be one of the most generous people I've ever had the pleasure of meeting.

My mum, my dad, Jamie and other brilliant individuals from this industry have shaped my cooking. But they've also done something else that they probably didn't intend. They've all made me very, very greedy. I adore cooking, but I can categorically say I like eating even more.

Everything I do in the kitchen is driven by the desire to eat, and the quicker I can get a great dish cooked and into my mouth, the happier I am.

For me, you don't need a rock-solid understanding of classic techniques to turn out a proper crowd-pleasing dish. You just need some straightforward instructions, a few cheat sheets, and a desire to create satisfying, craveable food.

My incurable greediness has led to the creation of this book. Food is one of life's greatest pleasures, but there's also an enormous amount of joy to be had from knowing you've just put great stuff into your body that will actually do you good.

The recipes in this book are all about satisfying both of those primal needs. Easy, replicable, lip-smackingly delicious and craveable dishes that will brighten the rainiest, most stressful day *and* leave you safe in the knowledge that you've just fed your body with all the things it needs, without your brain ever noticing.

This book is me through and through: I want to have my cake and eat it – and now you can too.

Brunch

The best gossip happens at brunch. The best life advice is dished out when it's a bottomless brunch. And the best long-overdue catch-ups start at brunch and end somewhere around midnight.

Every time I am back in my home town, I book in brunch with the girls. Brunch is the only meal that gives you enough time in the morning to make yourself presentable and enough hours in the day to put the world to rights with the people you love.

But you can't share good stories over bad food, so here are some brilliant recipes that are just as delicious as the conversation you're about to tuck into.

Creamy Masala Scrambled Eggs

SERVES 4 · TAKES 20 MINUTES

My husband makes the best scrambled eggs. Creamy, velvety ribbons served on a thin seeded bagel is me waking up on the right side of the bed. These extra-special scrambled eggs are set to start your day right, too.

1 tsp olive oil
1 brown onion, finely chopped
Pinch of salt
2 beef tomatoes, finely chopped
2 garlic cloves, crushed
1 red chilli, finely chopped
2 tsp garam masala
1 tsp ground turmeric
8 large free-range eggs
2 tbsp reduced-fat crème fraîche

TO SERVE
Sourdough bread, toasted
Chopped coriander (cilantro)

Add the oil to a frying pan over a low–medium heat. Add your onion and salt and soften for 4–5 minutes, turning it translucent but not colouring it. Next add your tomatoes, garlic, chilli, garam masala and turmeric. Turn down the heat to low and cook gently for 10 minutes until fragrant and well mingled.

Beat your eggs in a bowl before adding them to the pan – still over a low heat. Keep stirring constantly, turning the eggs into smooth, vibrant scrambles. Finish by stirring in the crème fraîche. Serve on sourdough toast, sprinkled with coriander.

Poached Eggs with Cheat's Hollandaise and Spinach

SERVES 4 · TAKES 20 MINUTES

Hollandaise is a sauce that requires a lot of patience. We rarely make it for visiting friends and family, as it often involves being stuck in the kitchen with an aching arm, the sauce constantly teetering on the brink of splitting. I'm a sucker for anything that gets me to the eating part as quickly as possible, and the speed and simplicity of this version (and the fact it doesn't have a block of butter in it) makes it a winner.

4–8 large free-range eggs (1 or 2 per person)
4 large handfuls of baby spinach
4 English muffins, split and toasted

FOR THE HOLLANDAISE SAUCE
Squeeze of lemon juice
200g (7oz) 0% fat thick Greek yogurt
1 tsp Dijon mustard
½ tsp paprika
3 large free-range egg yolks
Pinch of salt

For the hollandaise sauce, chuck everything into a bain marie (a bowl suspended over boiling water, see Notes) and whisk for about 10 minutes, until heated through. The sauce should loosen and be easily spoon-able. Season to taste with a little more salt, remove from the heat and set aside.

Crack your eggs carefully into a pan of simmering water and poach them for 2–3 minutes so the whites hold their shape but the centre is still runny.

To quickly wilt your spinach, pop it in a colander set over the sink and pour boiling water from the kettle over it. Allow it to cool a little before squeezing out any excess moisture. Divide the spinach between your toasted muffins and pop on your poached eggs before drenching in the warmed hollandaise. Absolutely delicious!

NOTES

To make a bain marie, choose a heatproof bowl that is larger than your saucepan. Simmer your water in the saucepan, ensuring the bowl is suspended above and not in contact with the water. This creates a gentle and uniform heat around your food, which is brilliant for delicate dishes such as custard, sauces, melted chocolate and eggs.

You can turn your hollandaise into a cheat's béarnaise sauce by simply sautéing finely sliced shallots and adding these to your sauce, along with chopped fresh tarragon.

Fresh eggs are best for poaching, as the whites are thick and closely surround the yolks, helping them keep their shape. However, the fresher the egg the harder it is to peel, making your older eggs perfect for the Caesar Salad on page 76.

Baked Breakfast Scotch Egg with Homemade Ketchup

MAKES 4 SUPER-SIZED SCOTCH EGGS
TAKES 50 MINUTES

The first time I realized that Scotch eggs weren't just for spring picnics was at a stall in Borough Market in London. We had been enjoying a few pints at a local brewery and wandered (or stumbled) into the food market later into the night. We had plans for dinner but needed a little sobering slice of something. I glanced at the Scotch eggs – the classic was there, but there were new, incredible combinations I'd never tried before. Black pudding Scotch egg! Smoked bacon and Cheddar! Spiced lentils and beetroot! They had 'next levelled' the humble Scotch egg, and now I'm going to do the same...

4 large free-range eggs

60g (2¼oz) mushrooms, torn

½ red onion, cut into chunks

400g (14oz) lean minced (ground) pork

½ x 400g (14oz) can of cannellini beans, drained and rinsed

1 tsp mustard

½ bunch of parsley, finely chopped

1½ tsp salt

½ tsp ground white pepper

Ketchup or musatrd 'mayo', to serve (see overleaf for homemade)

FOR THE COATING

150g (5½oz) plain (all-purpose) flour, seasoned with salt and black pepper

2 large free-range eggs

150g (5½oz) wholemeal (wholewheat) breadcrumbs (freshly blitzed bread is best)

1 red-skinned potato, grated and squeezed of excess moisture

Begin by boiling your eggs. Bring a pan of water to the boil, add the eggs, bring back to the boil, then simmer for 5 minutes. Remove and plunge them into ice-cold water (this will stop the cooking process). Carefully peel and set them aside.

Preheat the oven to 260°C (240°C fan/500°F/ gas 10) – or as hot as your oven will go if it doesn't reach that temperature.

Add your mushrooms and onion to a blender and blitz, then add the pork, beans, mustard, parsley, salt and pepper. Whizz together until combined. If you don't have a blender (or can't be bothered to get it out) then you can finely chop everything and mush it together by hand.

Divide the mixture into 4 equal balls, then flatten each one. Place a soft-boiled egg in the middle of each and carefully wrap the meat around it, sealing it in.

To coat, add your seasoned flour to one bowl. Crack the eggs into another bowl and whisk. Combine your breadcrumbs and grated potato in a third bowl. This is your pané line-up!

Roll your meat-covered egg in the seasoned flour, then in the egg and finally in the breadcrumbs and potato, giving it a light press to get as much crumb as possible to adhere to the egg. You are welcome to repeat the egg-and-breadcrumb step again for a thicker crust.

Place on a baking tray lined with baking paper and bake for 15 minutes before turning over and cooking for a final 10–15 minutes, until golden and the sausagemeat is cooked through (the juices will run clear and there is no pink meat).

Serve warm with homemade ketchup and/or mustard 'mayo' (overleaf).

Tomato Ketchup

MAKES 260ML (9FL OZ/1 CUP)

250g (9oz) passata (puréed, strained tomatoes)

2 tbsp tomato paste

2 tbsp apple cider vinegar

1 tsp onion granules

1 tsp garlic granules

½ tsp brown sugar

Put everything in a saucepan over a low–medium heat and cook for 10–15 minutes until reduced and smooth. Taste and season. Once cooled a little, I like to pop mine in a blender for an extra-smooth sauce.

Decant into a sterilized jar and store in the fridge for up to 4 weeks.

Mustard 'Mayo'

MAKES 260ML (9FL OZ/1 CUP)

150g (5½oz) low-fat Greek yogurt

50g (1¾oz) light mayonnaise

2 tsp Dijon mustard

Juice of ½ lemon

Salt and cracked black pepper

Mix the yogurt, mayonnaise and mustard in a bowl until well combined, then add the lemon juice and stir until smooth. Season to taste with salt and pepper.

Make fresh and eat within 3 days.

Light Leek and Feta Omelette Cups

MAKES 12 · TAKES 30 MINUTES

My nephews don't stop eating. It must be a genetic thing. They could polish off a family dinner and still wither on the sofa, feigning 'starvation'. My sister-in-law is a genius at having an arsenal of snacks stored for said 'emergencies', but there's nothing childish about these.

1 courgette (zucchini)
1 leek, finely chopped
½ tsp olive oil
8 large free-range eggs
3 tbsp milk
½ bunch of dill, finely chopped
100g (3½oz) feta, crumbled
Grating of fresh nutmeg
Low-calorie oil spray
Salt

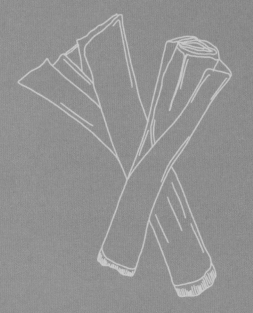

Preheat the oven to 210°C (190°C fan/410°F/ gas 6–7).

Begin by grating your courgette (skin on, just remove the stalk). Sprinkle with a little salt and set aside for 5 minutes, then pop your grated courgette into a clean tea (dish) towel or kitchen paper and give it a squeeze over the sink to drain it of excess moisture.

Meanwhile, add the leek to a frying pan over a medium–low heat with the oil and a pinch of salt. Cook for 3–5 minutes until softened. Allow to cool a little before you move on with the next step.

In a large bowl, whisk your eggs and milk until smooth, then add in your leek, courgette, dill, feta and nutmeg and mix until combined.

Spray a 12-hole muffin tray with low-calorie oil spray (if you have a silicone muffin tray, it'll be even better to ensure these cheeky treats don't stick!). Divide your mixture evenly between the holes.

We're going to cook this using a water bath. Grab a high-sided roasting tin or dish. Place your muffin tray inside the roasting tin and pour boiling water into the tin to surround the muffin tray, being careful not to let the water come over the top of the tray.

Pop it all in the oven and bake for 20 minutes, until set.

NOTES

To store, allow your omelette cups to cool completely before placing them in an airtight container. They will store in the fridge for 4 days and can be eaten cold or reheated in an 800W microwave for 40 seconds per cup.

Gooey Summer Berry and Ricotta Stuffed French Toast

SERVES 4 · TAKES 30 MINUTES

We always called this 'eggy bread' growing up and it was well and truly a weekend treat. The most standout French toast I've ever seen was in a New Jersey diner with my family. My cousin ordered it, and what was delivered was the equivalent of a loaf of bread, piled high with bacon and whipped cream and dripping with maple syrup. I think this recipe will make you feel a lot better than he did later that day...

FOR THE BERRY COMPOTE
200ml (7fl oz/scant 1 cup) orange juice
250g (9oz) frozen summer berries
2 tsp brown sugar

FOR THE FRENCH TOAST
160g (5¾oz) ricotta
4 very thick slices of sourdough bread
2 large free-range eggs
100ml (3½fl oz/scant ½ cup) skimmed milk
    (or dairy-free alternative)
1 tsp ground cinnamon
1 tsp vanilla bean paste (or extract)
Zest of 1 orange
Low-calorie oil spray, for frying

TO SERVE
0% fat Greek yogurt

Begin by making your summer berry compote. Pop all the ingredients in a saucepan and bring to the boil. Reduce the heat to low and simmer for 15–20 minutes, stirring continuously, until the berries have thawed and thickened with the orange juice into a glossy sauce.

Let the compote cool to room temperature, then mix half the compote with the ricotta until the berries are evenly dispersed.

Cut a pocket into each slice of sourdough (I find it easiest to put the berry ricotta into a piping/pastry bag at this point) and fill each of your pockets with the filling.

Whisk the eggs, milk, cinnamon, vanilla and orange zest together in a wide dish and submerge your filled bread in the liquid. Give the filled bread a flip so it is fully coated.

Lightly spray a large frying pan with cooking spray and add your soaked bread (in batches depending on the size of your pan and bread slices). Cook for 3–4 minutes until golden brown, then flip and repeat on the other side.

Serve with a dollop of Greek yogurt and the remaining berry compote on the side.

NOTES

Sugar isn't the enemy, but quantity is where we take control of it for the good of our health: 30g (1oz) free sugars a day is the recommended limit.

You can make the compote in advance and store it in the fridge for up to a week – any leftovers are delightful poured over other morning (or dessert) treats like pancakes or porridge.

Secret Spinach Scotch Pancakes with a Blueberry Drizzle

SERVES 4 (MAKES 8–10 PANCAKES)
TAKES 20 MINUTES

Our family friends always host pancake day. With an open-house policy, there are always four pans on the go to feed the never-ending stream of children and adults who pop in when they know the batter is fresh and the pancakes are flipping. When I'm scoffing down my ninth pancake of the day, I'd be feeling smug if it was one of these.

100g (3½oz) self-raising flour

40g (1½oz) rolled (porridge) oats

1 tbsp caster (superfine) sugar

1 tsp baking powder

Pinch of salt

120g (4¼oz) baby spinach

100ml (3½fl oz/scant ½ cup) skimmed milk (or dairy-free alternative)

2 large free-range eggs

Low-calorie oil spray, for frying

0% fat Greek yogurt, to serve

FOR THE BLUEBERRY DRIZZLE
200g (7oz) frozen blueberries

Juice of ½ lemon

2 tbsp maple syrup

Put all the ingredients for the blueberry drizzle into a saucepan and simmer lightly until the berries begin to burst. Keep it blipping away until glossy and oozy and ready to pour over your stunning pancakes.

Meanwhile, add your flour, oats, sugar, baking powder and salt to a blender and blitz until the oats are finely chopped and smoothed into the flour. Empty into a bowl. In the blender, blitz your spinach, milk and eggs together until you have a smooth liquid. Whisk your wet and dry mixtures together into a smooth batter.

Spritz a non-stick frying pan with oil spray and add 2–3 tablespoons of batter per pancake into the pan. If you have a large frying pan you'll be able to cook a few pancakes at a time. Cook for 1–2 minutes until bubbles form on the surface. Flip and repeat on the other side.

Serve with a dollop of yogurt and the blueberry drizzle poured over.

Poached Eggs in
Spicy Tomato and Bean Sauce

SERVES 4 · TAKES 35 MINUTES

I knew I'd reached the next stage of life when our friends started hosting lunches and not just plotting to meet at the pub and stumble home. The next, next stage of life is when your friends set aside the bacon sarnies in favour of my nourishing take on shakshuka.

2 red onions, halved and finely sliced
    (into half-moons)
4 red (bell) peppers, deseeded
    and sliced into thin strips
1 tbsp olive oil
4 garlic cloves, crushed
1 tsp ground cumin
1 tsp cayenne pepper
1 tsp smoked paprika
1 x 415g (14oz) can of baked beans
1 x 400g (14oz) can of plum tomatoes
100ml (3½fl oz/scant ½ cup) water
200g (7oz) spinach
4 large free-range eggs
2 tbsp 0% fat Greek yogurt
Small bunch of basil, leaves finely sliced
1 red chilli, finely sliced
Salt and ground black pepper

Add the red onions and peppers to a large frying pan with the oil. Cook over a medium heat for 5–6 minutes until soft and translucent, then add the garlic, cumin, cayenne and smoked paprika. Cook for 2–3 minutes until fragrant and everything has muddled together.

Pour in your baked beans, plum tomatoes (giving these a squeeze as you add them) and water and simmer for 10–12 minutes.

Pile on your spinach and stir through to wilt, then add salt and pepper to taste. Create 4 little divots in the mixture and crack an egg into each one. Put a lid on the pan and cook over a low heat for 6–7 minutes until the eggs are done.

Swirl the yogurt around the eggs, sprinkle with the basil and top with the red chilli.

NOTES

If you don't like baked beans, you can switch them out for another can of plum tomatoes.

Easy Avocado Toast Served 3 Ways

EACH SERVES 2 · TAKES 5+ MINUTES

When we have friends come to stay, our default is to whip up a load of poached eggs, smash up some avocado and then display a plethora of delicious topping options. Think bowls dotted all over the table of feta, pomegranate, bacon, coriander, yogurt, toasted seeds, pickled veg and spoons for everyone to top their avocado toast exactly as they want to. Here are a few of my favourite combinations...

HIDDEN EGG AND AVOCADO SOURDOUGH TOAST

Handful of cherry tomatoes (12–14), halved

1 ripe avocado, peeled, halved and pitted

Juice of ½ lime

1 red chilli, finely chopped

2 slices of sourdough bread

Olive oil, for greasing

2 free-range eggs

Salt and ground black pepper

AVOCADO RYE TOAST WITH PICKLED VEG

1 carrot

Handful of radishes

2 tbsp apple cider vinegar

1 ripe avocado, peeled, halved and pitted

40g (1½oz) cottage cheese

Small pinch of ground cumin

4 slices of rye bread

Salt and ground black pepper

HIDDEN EGG AND AVOCADO SOURDOUGH TOAST

Sprinkle the halved tomatoes with a small pinch of salt, then sit them in a sieve (strainer) and leave them to drain off any excess liquid. This will intensify their flavour.

Mash your avocado using a fork and mix in the lime juice and chilli, and a small pinch each of salt and pepper.

Using a 7cm (2¾in) round cookie cutter (or cut around a glass), remove a circle from the centre of your bread slices (you don't need these cut-out circles in this recipe, so turn into breadcrumbs and store in the freezer for another use, such as for the Scotch eggs on page 14). Place the centre-less bread slices in a lightly oiled non-stick frying pan and toast for 1–2 minutes before flipping and cracking an egg into each hole. Fry for 2–3 minutes, then turn the heat down and cover with a lid until the whites are set but the yolks still have a jiggle.

Smother the toast with the avocado and sprinkle on your cherry tomatoes. Slice for a delightful surprise!

AVOCADO RYE TOAST WITH PICKLED VEG

Using either a mandoline or a swivel peeler, shave your carrot and radishes into thin strips/discs and pop into a bowl with a pinch of salt and the vinegar. Give everything a good squeeze and allow it to sit and pickle for 15–20 minutes.

Put your avocado and cottage cheese in a separate bowl and mash together. Season with salt and pepper and the cumin.

Toast the rye bread and slather on the avocado mixture. Top with your quick pickled veggies (giving them a squeeze beforehand).

AVOCADO AND CRUSHED PEA WITH SALMON ON WHOLEMEAL TOAST

100g (3½oz) frozen petits pois
1 ripe avocado, peeled, halved and pitted
Juice of ½ lemon
Small handful of fresh dill, finely chopped
2 slices of wholemeal (wholewheat) bread
60g (2¼oz) smoked salmon
Ground black pepper

AVOCADO AND CRUSHED PEA WITH SALMON ON WHOLEMEAL TOAST

Blanch your peas for 1–2 minutes in lightly salted water, then drain. Add two thirds of the peas to a bowl with the avocado, lemon juice and dill, then crush and mash everything together.

Toast the wholemeal bread and top with the avocado mixture. Sprinkle over the remaining peas, layer on the salmon and finish with a good grind of black pepper.

NOTES

Invest in a good-quality non-stick pan and you'll end up needing to use less oil.

· pick me up ·

Moreish Stuffed Dates 3 Ways

EACH RECIPE MAKES 12 STUFFED DATES · TAKES 10+ MINUTES

We're that family who buys dates at Christmas and questions, 'Why don't we buy these all year round?' Unlike the marzipan florentines and coconut chocolates that get rejected each year – only to be served the following Christmas despite their dwindling 'best-before' date – these sweet treats bring joy to me every day of the year.

12 dates (preferably Medjool)

FOR THE CLASSIC
6 tsp crunchy peanut butter
60g (2¼oz) dark (semisweet)
    chocolate (minimum 70% cocoa)
Flaky sea salt

FOR THE SAVOURY
12 basil leaves
6 tsp low-fat cream cheese
4 slices of Parma ham, each cut into 3 strips

FOR THE MAKE AHEAD
2 red apples
1–2cm (½–¾in) piece of fresh ginger,
    peeled and finely grated
1 tsp ground cinnamon
2 tbsp water
12 walnut halves

Use a sharp knife to cut along one side of the dates and remove the stone (pit) to create a neat little pocket for your filling. Be careful as you handle them so as not to squish them out of shape.

For the **Classic**, add ½ teaspoon of peanut butter to each date and close the pocket back up. Melt your chocolate in a heatproof bowl placed over a saucepan of simmering water over a medium heat (a bain marie – see page 13). Add your chocolate to the bowl and, once it has melted, dip one end of your stuffed dates into it and place on a tray lined with baking paper. Sprinkle with a little flaky sea salt and pop in the fridge to firm up.

For the **Savoury**, lay a basil leaf inside each date then spoon in ½ teaspoon of cream cheese. Wrap up each date with the Parma ham strips. These can be eaten immediately or stored in the fridge until later, ready to be served as comforting canapés.

For the **Make Ahead**, core but don't peel the apples (there's so much goodness in the skin) and grate them. Set a pan over a medium heat and add the apples, ginger, cinnamon and water. Give it a stir, then cover the pan and cook for 3–4 minutes. Stir gently and often, covering between stirs, until your apples are soft. Add 1 teaspoon of stewed apple to each pitted date, then insert a walnut half into each. Pop in the fridge to set a little and then tuck in. The stewed apple will make more than you need for this recipe – store the leftovers in the fridge and use as a porridge topper or stirred into yogurt.

NOTES

Your dates can be stored in the fridge in an airtight container for about 5 days, though for the best flavours and textures stuff them fresh.

Stuffed dates freeze well. Freeze them on a baking tray until solid, then they can be tossed into an airtight container and stored in the freezer for up to 3 months. Allow them to thaw in the fridge.

Blueberry Bursting Breakfast Muffins

MAKES 12 · TAKES 40 MINUTES

When I was growing up, my parents seemed to keep befriending people with sons. Having an older brother, I had become well versed in wrestling, but when I didn't fancy being held in a WWE-style sleeper hold for the umpteenth time, I would retire to the kitchen and spend time baking cakes with the mums, giving us all some much-needed testosterone-free time.

180g (6¼oz) plain wholemeal (all-purpose wholewheat) flour
100g (3½oz) rolled (porridge) oats
1 tsp ground cinnamon
2 tsp baking powder
1 tsp bicarbonate of soda (baking soda)
2 large free-range eggs
4 tbsp light brown sugar
200g (7oz) 0% fat Greek yogurt
1 apple, grated (keep skin on)
1 banana, mashed
150g (5½oz) frozen blueberries

Preheat the oven to 220°C (200°C fan/425°F/gas 7). Line a muffin tray with 12 paper cases.

In a large mixing bowl, combine the flour, oats, cinnamon, baking powder and bicarbonate of soda.

In a separate bowl, whisk together the eggs and sugar until smooth. Add the yogurt, grated apple and mashed banana and stir until well combined.

Pour the wet ingredients into the dry ingredients and mix until just combined. Gently fold in the frozen blueberries, then divide the mixture evenly between the muffin cases.

Bake for 15–20 minutes or until a toothpick inserted into the centre of a muffin comes out clean.

Remove from the oven and allow to cool in the tin for 5 minutes before transferring to a wire rack to cool completely.

Crispy Chicken with Cheesy Cauliflower Waffles

SERVES 4 · TAKES 40 MINUTES

I can't quite remember when it clicked that I love the combo of sweet and savoury together. Now I always have grapes with my cheese, melon wrapped in salty ham, and maple syrup on my fried chicken! It's a flavour combination that just works.

120g (4½oz) cornflakes
2 tsp paprika
½ tsp salt
Pinch of ground black pepper
30g (1oz) plain (all-purpose) flour
2 large free-range eggs
4 boneless, skinless chicken breasts
Maple syrup, to serve

FOR THE CAULIFLOWER WAFFLES
1 medium-sized cauliflower
2 large free-range eggs
250ml (9fl oz/1 cup) milk
200g (7oz) self-raising flour
70g (2¼oz) Parmesan, grated
Pinch each of salt and ground black pepper
Olive oil, for frying

Preheat the oven to 200°C (180°C fan/400°F/gas 6).

Crush the cornflakes into small pieces and mix with the paprika, salt and pepper in a small bowl. Place the flour in another shallow bowl. Beat the eggs in a third shallow bowl. Dip each chicken breast in the flour, shaking off any excess. Then dip it in the beaten egg until fully coated. Finally, coat the chicken in the cornflake mixture, pressing it onto the chicken to make sure it sticks. Place on a baking tray lined with baking paper and bake for 20–25 minutes or until the chicken is cooked through and the coating is golden and crispy.

Meanwhile, dice the cauliflower into small florets and pulse in a food processor until it resembles rice. Place the cauliflower rice in a microwave-safe bowl, cover and microwave for 5 minutes. If you don't have a microwave, give it a quick blanch in boiling water for 2–3 minutes, then drain. Let the cauliflower cool for a few minutes before squeezing out excess water using a clean tea (dish) towel.

In a mixing bowl, combine the cauliflower rice, eggs, milk, flour, Parmesan, salt and pepper and mix until everything is fully incorporated. Heat a non-stick frying pan over a medium heat and add a small drizzle of olive oil. Scoop 2 ladlefuls of the cauliflower batter into the pan and flatten them out using a spatula. Cook for about 3–4 minutes on each side or until golden brown and crispy. Repeat the process with the remaining batter. (Alternatively, cook in your waffle iron.)

Serve the cauliflower waffles topped with the crispy chicken, then drizzle over some maple syrup

NOTES

You can make the waffle batter ahead and freeze it for up to 3 months. Thaw the batter overnight in the fridge (or for at least 4 hours) before using.

The best way to reheat these waffles is in a toaster for 2 minutes – they should crisp up nicely again.

Comforting Classics

Picture a quintessential British pub tucked
away on a cobbled street. Just inside
the door, jackets are hung up, dripping
gently after an inevitable downpour. You
find a spot on a squishy leather sofa, the
comforting scent of the crackling fire
enveloping you as you sit back with a glass
of something lovely in your hand.

These dishes would all be
on the menu of that pub.

Heartiness and generosity are a must with
these comforting classics, but with a few
clever twists you can capture that peaceful
bliss at home and know you're doing your
body a whole load of good in the process.

Seeded Soda Bread Cheese Toastie

MAKES 1 LOAF / 4–6 TOASTIES
TAKES 1+ HOURS

Bread is the Phantom (of the Opera...
yes, I studied theatre) of the food world:
misunderstood and deemed a villain without
really getting to know it. Truth be told, the best
bread is the bread you make yourself, but who
has the time? You. You do.

FOR THE SEEDED SODA BREAD
350g (12oz) wholemeal (wholewheat) flour,
    plus extra for dusting
150g (5½oz) plain (all-purpose) flour
85g (3oz) mixed seeds and chopped nuts
    (flax, pumpkin, pine nuts, pistachios, etc.)
1 tsp salt
1½ tsp bicarbonate of soda (baking soda)
2½ tbsp lemon juice
500g (17oz) low-fat plain yogurt

FOR THE FILLINGS
Butter, for spreading
Choose one of the following combinations:
- Applewood smoked cheese + kimchi
- Mature Cheddar + finely sliced red onion
  scrunched with a splash of vinegar
  + finely diced dried apricots
- Ricotta + sliced fresh figs + Parma ham

Preheat the oven to 200°C (180°C fan/400°F/
gas 6). Line a baking tray with baking paper
and dust with flour.

Mix your flours, seeds and nuts, salt and
bicarbonate of soda in a bowl. In a separate
bowl, mix your lemon juice and yogurt, then
combine this with the dry mixture until you have
a sticky dough – use a knife to initially bring
the ingredients together and finish by briefly
kneading it with your hands. Shape it into a
rounded loaf, but try not to handle it too much,
so you don't end up with a dense bread.

Pop the dough onto the prepared baking tray and
score a deep cross into the top, almost two-thirds
of the way down. Bake for 45–50 minutes until
golden and it makes a good hollow tapping sound
on the underside. Leave to cool.

To make the toasties, cut 2 thick slices of bread
for each sandwich. Fill with your chosen filling,
then lightly butter the outside of your sandwiches.

Heat a large frying pan over a medium heat and
add your sandwich (it's best to cook them one at
a time). Use a heavy saucepan to weigh down your
delicious soon-to-be toastie, helping it become
golden and crisp and ensuring the heat reaches
your filling and helps it ooze. Cook for 2–3
minutes, then flip and repeat on the other side.

NOTES

If you want to make the bread with entirely white
flour (rather than a mix of white and wholemeal
flour) it may be helpful to use less flour than
the amount called for in the recipe, because
white flour absorbs less liquid than wholemeal
flour, and using too much may result in a dry or
crumbly texture. A good rule of thumb is to start
by substituting 75–80% of the wholemeal flour
with white flour and adjusting as needed.

Mince and Onion Flatbread Pasty

SERVES 4 · TAKES 50 MINUTES

Imagine a cabin hidden in Cornish farmland, two terrier puppies drying off from a frolic on the beach, our phones desperately searching for signal so we can watch the latest box set we're obsessed with. Add these quick and easy pasties and you have my perfect Saturday night by the coast.

100g (3½oz) sweet potato, unpeeled, chopped into 5mm (¼in) cubes

150g (5½oz) white potato, unpeeled, chopped into 5mm (¼in) cubes

½ brown onion, finely chopped

400g (14oz) lean minced (ground) beef

1 tsp ground black pepper

1½ tsp salt

½ tsp dried thyme (optional, for extra flavour)

200g (7oz) self-raising flour

1 tsp baking powder

200g (7oz) low-fat plain yogurt

2–3 tbsp water

1 large free-range egg, beaten

Preheat the oven to 180°C (160°C fan/350°F/gas 4).

In a bowl, mix the potatoes, onion, beef, pepper, salt and thyme (if using), ensuring the beef is evenly crumbled throughout the rest of the ingredients. Set aside.

Mix the flour and baking powder in a separate bowl. Add the yogurt and bring together with a fork. Add enough water to bring the ingredients into a rough dough, then briefly knead until smooth – try not to overwork it or your bread will be tough. Divide the dough into 4 equal pieces and roll each piece into a long oblong about 2mm (⅛in) thick.

Divide your filling mixture equally into 4, then place each portion on one half of a rolled dough piece. Brush the edges of the dough with the beaten egg and fold the dough over so the filling is sealed inside and you have what resembles a pasty.

To crimp the edge of each pasty, push down on the sealed edge with your finger and twist the seam over. When you've crimped along the edge, fold the end corners underneath. Brush the whole thing with egg and pierce the top with two small knife incisions, to create steam holes – this will help your filling cook and keep your pasty crisp.

Place on a baking tray and bake for 30 minutes or until your pasties are golden and the underside is crisp, too.

Bang Bang Smash Burgers

SERVES 4 · TAKES 30 MINUTES

The best kind of burger leaves a trail of destruction on your plate and face. If your fingers and chin aren't dripping with delicious juices while you frantically work to catch the condiments trying to slide out the side, then something isn't quite right.

2 bundles of rice noodles
8 romaine or iceberg lettuce leaves
Salt and ground black pepper

FOR THE SMASH BURGER PATTIES
500g (1lb 2oz) lean minced (ground) beef
1 carrot, grated
1 tsp garlic granules
1 tsp onion granules
¼ tsp ground black pepper
1 free-range egg
Olive oil, for frying

FOR THE BANG BANG SLAW
½ small green cabbage, very thinly sliced
½ small red cabbage, very thinly sliced
1 large carrot, finely grated
60g (2¼oz) 0% fat Greek yogurt
2 tbsp honey
2 tbsp Sriracha sauce
Juice of 1 lime

To make the slaw, combine the green and red cabbage and carrot in a large bowl. In a separate bowl, whisk together the yogurt, honey, Sriracha and lime juice. Pour the dressing over the cabbage and carrot mixture and toss until everything is evenly coated. Season with salt and pepper to taste. Store in the fridge until ready to serve.

Cook your rice noodles according to the packet instructions. Drain and rinse through with hot water.

Combine the burger patty ingredients except the oil in a large mixing bowl and mix well until evenly combined. Divide the mixture into 8 equal portions and shape them into balls.

Preheat a frying pan over a high heat. Once hot, add a small amount of oil to the pan.

In batches, so you don't overcrowd the pan, place the balls in the pan and use a spatula to smash them down into very thin patties. Cook for about 2–3 minutes on each side or until they are browned and crispy.

Use one of the lettuce leaves as the bottom 'bun' of your burger. Top with 1 smash burger, then a portion of noodles, then another smash burger and finally your slaw. Sandwich with another lettuce leaf and tuck in. Make sure you have a napkin, as this is about to get very messy.

COMFORTING CLASSICS

Macaroni and Cannellini Cheese with a Roasted Cauliflower Crust

SERVES 4 · TAKES 35 MINUTES

The first thing I ever learned to cook was a cheese sauce. The carnage of pots and pans littering the kitchen surface would fade into the background as I drowned penne pasta and sliced-up packet ham in this velvety sauce. Creamy and cheesy to its core, I've improved this version many times over the years and, to my parents' delight, have become far better at washing up after myself in the process.

½ large cauliflower, ideally with leaves
1 tsp olive oil
300g (10½oz) dried macaroni
1 x 400g (14oz) can of cannellini beans, drained and rinsed
250ml (9fl oz/1 cup) vegetable stock
100g (3½oz) Cheddar cheese, grated
1 tsp wholegrain mustard
Salt and ground white pepper

Preheat the oven to 200°C (180°C fan/400°F/gas 6).

Begin by pulling the leaves off your cauliflower half and slicing it in half again (so you have 2 quarters). Chop one of the quarters into florets and bung in a roasting dish with the leaves. Pour over the oil, season with salt and white pepper and roast for 20 minutes, tossing halfway through.

Meanwhile, get the macaroni cooking in a pan of boiling, salted water according to the packet instructions – we want al dente!

Finely chop the remaining cauliflower quarter, pop it into a pan with the cannellini beans and stock, bring to the boil, then simmer for 6 minutes. Transfer the contents of the pan to a blender and whizz until smooth. Add the mixture back to the pan and set over a low heat. Add 80g (2¾oz) of your grated Cheddar, the mustard and ½ teaspoon each of salt and white pepper. Warm through until the cheese has fully melted.

Add the drained macaroni to the sauce and fold everything together. Tip everything into a baking dish and top with the roasted cauliflower florets and leaves. Sprinkle over the remaining grated cheese, then pop it under the grill (broiler) until your cheese turns golden. Serve immediately.

NOTES

Pasta is part of a good diet. It's made from grain, is a good source of energy and can give you fibre, too. It's all about balancing the choice of pasta with what you top it with. Many also say there's no place for cheese in a heart-healthy diet, but there's room for everything in moderation.

I like using white pepper where I want the warmth but not necessarily too much 'peppery' flavour. I use black pepper when I want that spicy, fruity pepper taste.

Crispy Chicken Wings with a Blue Cheese Dip

SERVES 4 (MAKES 10–12 WINGS)
TAKES 2+ HOURS

When I was in the throes of my London partying prime, all I ever wanted at the end of a night out was a bucket of crispy chicken wings to take to bed with me. Tuck into these for that same glow of delicious comfort... bed optional.

1kg (2lb 3oz) chicken wings
4 tbsp low-fat plain yogurt
2 tsp smoked paprika
2 tsp garlic granules
2 tsp chilli flakes (or to taste)
2 tbsp Worcestershire sauce
Oil, for greasing
150g (5½oz) cornflakes
Salt and ground black pepper

FOR THE BLUE CHEESE DIP
100g (3½oz) 0% fat Greek yogurt
60g (2¼oz) blue cheese, crumbled
1 tsp white wine vinegar
1 tsp garlic granules

Add your chicken wings to a large bowl with the yogurt, smoked paprika, garlic, chilli flakes, Worcestershire sauce and 1 teaspoon each of salt and pepper, then stir to give them a good coating. Cover and marinate for at least 2 hours, but ideally overnight, in the fridge.

Preheat the oven to 240°C (220°C fan/475°F/gas 9). Line a baking tray and grease with a little oil.

Crush the cornflakes in a bowl and season with salt and pepper. Take your yogurt-coated chicken and coat it in the crushed cornflakes, then spread the coated chicken out evenly on the prepared baking tray. Roast in the oven for 20 minutes, then flip and roast for a further 10 minutes.

For the blue cheese dip, simply mix the ingredients together in a bowl.

Serve the chicken wings with the creamy blue cheese dip.

COMFORTING CLASSICS

Meaty Mushroom Burger

SERVES 6 · TAKES 1 HOUR 30 MINUTES

In 2018 I was in LA – birthplace of the Beyond Burger and my first experience of a veggie burger that wasn't a dry patty made of beans and cardboard and served with lashings of ketchup to insert some sort of moisture. This is my version of a perfect veggie burger – juicy, hearty and simple to create.

300g (10½oz) chestnut (cremini) mushrooms, cut into 1cm (½in) chunks

Pinch of salt

3 tbsp soy sauce (preferably dark)

2 tbsp olive oil

1 small red onion, finely diced

3–4 tbsp water

180g (6¼oz) cooked pearl barley (see Note overleaf)

140g (5oz) extra-firm tofu, pressed and crumbled into pieces the size of the mushrooms

75g (2½oz) walnuts, finely chopped

40g (1½oz) fine dry breadcrumbs

1 large free-range egg

1 tbsp balsamic vinegar

2½ tsp dried oregano

2½ tsp garlic granules

2½ tsp smoked paprika

¼ tsp ground white pepper (or black pepper if you don't have white)

TO SERVE

6 wholemeal (wholewheat) burger buns

Lettuce

Thinly sliced red onion

Sliced tomatoes

Low-fat mayonnaise

Sauté the mushrooms with the salt in a large (dry) non-stick frying pan over a medium–high heat, stirring occasionally until they release some liquid. When the liquid has cooked off and the mushrooms have started to turn golden, pour in the soy sauce and stir to coat the mushrooms. Tip the mushrooms into a large bowl and place the pan back over a medium heat.

Add 1 tablespoon of the oil to the pan, then add the onion and water, stirring to scrape up all the soy sauce residue. Cook until the onions have softened and the water has evaporated, around 5 minutes. Tip the onions into the same bowl as the mushrooms.

Add the cooked pearl barley, crumbled tofu, walnuts, breadcrumbs, egg, vinegar and all the dried herbs/spices to the mushroom and onion bowl and mix until fully combined.

Remove 260g (9¼oz/1½ cups) of the mixture and blend in a food processor to a coarse paste, stopping to scrape down the sides of the bowl a few times. Add this back into the bowl and mix.

Divide the mixture into 6 even balls and flatten them slightly on a lined baking tray. Chill in the fridge for a least an hour. Alternatively, these can be made in advance and stored, covered, in the fridge for up to 3 days.

To cook, heat the remaining tablespoon of oil in a large non-stick frying pan set over a medium heat. Add the burgers, 2 or 3 at a time depending on the size of your pan, and cook until deep golden underneath. Flip and cook until the other side is golden, then serve up in a burger bun with lettuce, onion, tomatoes and a swipe of mayo.

Recipe continues overleaf.

NOTES

If cooking your pearl barley from scratch, you'll need about 90g (3¼oz) dried pearl barley. Place it in a medium pot and cover with water. Add a pinch of salt and bring to the boil over a medium heat, then turn down to a simmer and cook for 20–30 minutes until cooked through but still retaining some bite. Drain and set aside to cool.

Store uncooked patties in an airtight container and freeze for up to 3 months. You can cook them from frozen in the same way you usually would. Just use a lower heat so they can defrost fully in the pan and expect to cook them for a few minutes longer to ensure they're warmed through. Alternatively, brush with oil and bake on a lined baking tray at 180°C (160°C fan/350°F/gas 4) for 20–30 minutes, flipping them over halfway through, until piping hot.

. pick me up .

Mini Roasted Jacket Potatoes Stuffed 2 Ways

SERVES 4 · TAKES 50 MINUTES

The mini version of anything is bound to put a smile on someone's face. These little new potatoes are baked so they're crispy on the outside and fluffy in the centre – a small snack filled with big flavours.

12 new potatoes (3 new potatoes per person), ideally all a similar size
2 tsp oil
Salt and ground black pepper

CANAPÉ CLASSIC
½ large cucumber, chopped into small cubes
120g (4¼oz) low-fat cream cheese
½ bunch of dill, finely chopped
120g (4¼oz) smoked salmon

MODERN BEETS
140g (5oz) ready-to-eat cooked beetroot (beets) in vinegar, chopped into small cubes
1 tsp harissa
120g (4¼oz) cottage cheese
60g (2¼oz) pine nuts
12 mint leaves, finely chopped

Preheat the oven to 210°C (190°C fan/410°F/ gas 6–7).

Chuck your potatoes, oil and a pinch of salt into a bowl and give the potatoes a toss so they're evenly coated. Spread them in a single layer on a baking tray, pop into the oven and bake for 40–45 minutes. Allow to cool a little before scoring them on top and gently opening them up a little, ready to be filled.

For the **canapé classic**, mix the cucumber with the cream cheese and dill and season with salt and pepper. Dollop this into your new potatoes, then top each with 10g (⅓oz) smoked salmon per potato.

For the **modern beets**, mix the beetroot with the harissa and cottage cheese, then taste and season. Spoon the mixture into your potatoes. Lightly toast your pine nuts in a dry pan set over a medium heat – give them a regular shuffle until they're golden. Sprinkle the toasted pine nuts on top of the potatoes and finish with some finely chopped mint leaves.

Lasagne with a Ricotta Bechamel and Pork Ragu

SERVES 6 · TAKES 2 HOURS

My nan's lasagne was wheeled out on a heated hostess trolley and – as with all her dishes – served with a vinaigrette-drenched salad. We would sit at our allocated spots with personalized napkin rings, and she'd bring out the good china. I love how even the simplest dishes make for the most special occasion. I never want to sacrifice the joy of a creamy bechamel, but this is often the deciding factor that tips a dish from weekday staple to weekend treat. Here's a clever little alternative, using cottage cheese and ricotta, that is no less delicious.

1 tbsp olive oil
1 brown onion, finely chopped
1 large carrot, finely chopped
1 celery stick, finely chopped
3 portobello mushrooms, finely chopped
4 garlic cloves, crushed
500g (1lb 2oz) lean minced (ground) pork
1 tbsp tomato paste
Small pinch of chilli flakes
½ tsp dried oregano
2 x 400g (14oz) cans of plum tomatoes
300g (10½oz) fresh lasagne sheets
300g (10½oz) spinach
Salt and ground black pepper

FOR THE WHITE SAUCE
160g (5½oz) ricotta
300g (10½oz) low-fat cottage cheese
60ml (2fl oz/¼ cup) skimmed milk
Zest of ¼ lemon
1 tbsp olive oil
Small handful of basil leaves, chopped

Heat the oil in a large pan over a low–medium heat, add the onion, carrot, celery, mushrooms and garlic and cook for 8–10 minutes, until soft. Remove from the pan and set aside.

Add the minced pork to the pan and cook, stirring, over a high heat for about 5 minutes, until golden. Add your veggies back to the pan along with the tomato paste, chilli flakes and oregano and cook for 2 minutes. Add the canned tomatoes, giving them a good squeeze as you add them. Then fill one-and-a-half of the cans with water and add that, too. Bring your ragu to a boil, then drop it to a simmer and cook for 45 minutes, stirring regularly, until it has thickened into a vibrant red sauce. Check the seasoning and add salt and pepper to taste.

Preheat the oven to 220°C (200°C fan/425°F/gas 7).

To make your white sauce, simply whip together your ricotta, cottage cheese, milk, lemon zest, oil and basil using a whisk or blender. Add salt and pepper to taste.

Now it's time to assemble. Grab an oven dish, about 23 x 33cm (9 x 13in). Begin with a portion of ragu, then add a layer of pasta, then a layer of spinach, and then spread over a generous dollop of white sauce (don't worry if it mingles with the spinach). Add another layer of pasta and repeat the process again until you have used up all your components. Be sure to finish on a layer of white sauce.

Cover the dish with foil and bake for 30 minutes, then remove the foil and cook for a further 20 minutes, until everything is golden and bubbling.

NOTES

Stored in an airtight container, leftover lasagne will keep in the fridge for up to 5 days. You can freeze your lasagne unbaked, then simply thaw it in the fridge overnight before cooking as per the recipe. If you've already cooked your lasagne, cool it, portion it and wrap each slice with cling film (plastic wrap), then freeze for up to 2 months.

Pink Cottage Pie

SERVES 4 · TAKES 1 HOUR 30 MINUTES

My parents instilled in me a love of food, but they also taught me to be a bit of a show off. This vibrant pink pie can be placed in the centre of the table with a theatricality that makes for as much enjoyment on the eyes as on the tastebuds!

1 brown onion, finely chopped

1 carrot, grated

2 tsp olive oil

2 tsp salt

250g (9oz) mushrooms, finely chopped (duxelles-style)

1 tbsp water

500g (1lb 2oz) lean minced (ground) beef

1 tbsp Worcestershire sauce

1½ tsp Dijon mustard

500ml (17fl oz/2 cups) beef stock

500g (1lb 2oz) potatoes, unpeeled, cut into 2.5cm (1in) chunks

250g (9oz) ready-to-eat cooked beetroot (beet), cut into 2.5cm (1in) chunks

3 heaped tbsp reduced-fat crème fraîche

Handful of chives, finely chopped

Add the onion and grated carrot to a large saucepan with the oil and 1 teaspoon of the salt. Cook over a low–medium heat for 8–10 minutes, to soften. Add the mushrooms and water and allow these to sweat for 2–3 minutes. Remove everything from the pan and set aside.

Now add the minced beef and cook over a high heat for 4–5 minutes, breaking up the mince with your spoon/spatula and ensuring everything is coloured and cooked through.

Deglaze the pan by adding a generous glug of boiling water and scraping off any bits stuck to the bottom. Add your veggies back to the pan with the Worcestershire sauce, 1 teaspoon of the mustard, and the beef stock. Simmer, uncovered, for 30–40 minutes, checking regularly to make sure it doesn't dry out, until it is reduced and thick. Tip into a pie dish.

Preheat the oven to 200°C (180°C fan/400°F/gas 6).

Add the potatoes and beetroot to a pan of boiling salted water and cook for 10–12 minutes, or until both are tender enough for a fork to press through with ease. Drain and add back to the empty pan with the crème fraîche and the remaining teaspoon of salt and ½ teaspoon of mustard. Mash until smooth and completely pink. Stir through the chives.

Spoon your pink mash over your pie filling and spread it out so your filling is covered. Bake in the oven for 25–30 minutes, or until your mash has slightly crisped on top. Serve with a side salad or freshly blanched greens.

NOTES

Half of the fibre of a potato comes from the skin, so keep those potatoes unpeeled!

Skinless Pork and Apple Sausages, Creamy Mash and Mushroom Gravy

SERVES 4 · TAKES 50 MINUTES

Sausages are snaffled at an extraordinary rate in our house and our usual mash is more butter than potato... to save us from ourselves at Chez Pix, we've switched to this delicious twist on one of our favourite comforting suppers!

1 slice of white bread, crusts removed

70ml (2¼fl oz/4½ tbsp) milk

500g (1lb 2oz) lean minced (ground) pork

1 tsp salt

½ tsp ground black pepper

1½ tsp wholegrain mustard

½ tsp dried sage

1 Granny Smith apple

1 tsp olive oil

FOR THE MASH

1kg (2lb 3oz) potatoes, peeled and cut into 5cm (2in) cubes

About 3 litres (6¼ pints) hot chicken stock

4 tbsp reduced-fat crème fraîche

FOR THE CREAMY GRAVY

1 tbsp olive oil

½ red onion, finely sliced into half rounds

250g (9oz) mixed mushrooms, torn up or sliced

200g (7oz) reduced-fat crème fraîche

NOTES

The process of using bread to tenderize meat is called 'panade' or 'panada'. The bread acts as a binding agent and helps retain moisture in the meat, resulting in a more tender and juicy texture.

Any remaining stock can be saved for other recipes. The starch released from the potatoes will add a velvety viscosity to soups, stews and gravies. Why not try it in my leek and potato soup (page 87) or minestrone (page 91). Leftover stock will last for 3–4 days in the fridge or up to 6 months if frozen.

Blitz the bread, milk, pork mince, salt and pepper in a food processor for 2 minutes. Stop when it clumps together into a big ball. Add the mustard and dried sage and give it one more quick blitz to incorporate. (Alternatively, you can do this by hand: put the bread in a mixing bowl, pour over the milk to soften it, then add your pork, salt, pepper, mustard and sage and knead the mixture together for 5–10 minutes until you start to feel an almost springy resistance to your pork.)

Grate the apple into a bowl, then squeeze out the juices (set the juices aside for your gravy later) and add the pulp to the sausage bowl. Mix well, then divide the mixture into 8 equal portions and roll each portion into a sausage shape.

Heat the oil in a frying pan over a medium heat, add the sausages and cook for 15–20 minutes, turning them regularly to get a golden outer crust.

Meanwhile, add the potatoes to a large pan and pour in enough chicken stock to generously cover them. Bring to the boil and boil for 12–15 minutes, or until tender enough for a fork to press through with ease. Drain over a heatproof bowl (retaining the stock for your gravy) then add the potatoes back to the empty pan with the crème fraîche. Mash until smooth then season with salt and pepper.

To make the gravy, add the oil and onions to a saucepan set over a medium heat and cook gently for about 20 minutes until soft and sticky. Add the mushrooms and continue to cook until they are tender and golden brown. Pour in 250–300ml (9–11fl oz/1–1¼ cups) of the reserved chicken stock and the reserved apple juices and bring the mixture to a simmer. Cook for a few minutes to allow the flavours to meld together, then stir in the crème fraîche until it is fully incorporated into the mixture. Add more stock if needed to reach your preferred gravy consistency.

Add a dollop of mash to each plate along with a couple of sausages, then spoon over the creamy gravy. Serve with your favourite greens.

COMFORTING CLASSICS

One-pan, No-split Carbonara

SERVES 2 · TAKES 20 MINUTES

When you marry into an Italian family, you learn to NEVER order the carbonara if it's made with cream (nor put chicken in pasta or on pizza, but that's a story for another time). Though this isn't an authentic carbonara, we're celebrating its simplicity with the proper ingredients – spaghetti, eggs and Parmesan.

2 slices of back bacon, finely sliced (if you want to be extra-healthy, remove the rind)
1 tsp olive oil
200g (7oz) dried spaghetti
2 tsp salt
2 large free-range eggs, beaten
80g (2¾oz) Parmesan, grated, plus extra to serve
1 tsp ground black pepper

Fry the bacon with the oil in a wide-based, deep-sided frying pan over a medium heat, until crispy. Remove the bacon, reserving the oil in the pan.

Add the spaghetti to the pan and cover with enough boiling water from the kettle so that it's *just* submerged. Add the salt and bring to the boil. Keep the pasta moving to avoid it sticking together and to massage the starch out to create a thick and glossy sauce. Keep cooking until your pasta is just short of al dente, topping up the water from the kettle if and when it's looking dry (I normally top up 2–3 times over the course of cooking).

Mix your beaten eggs and Parmesan together in a small bowl. Take the spaghetti pan off the heat, add the bacon back to the pan, then pour in the egg mixture. Work quickly to move the pasta and sauce around the pan, creating a velvety coating. Finish with a grind of fresh black pepper and then serve in bowls with extra parmesan grated over, if you like.

NOTES

To check your pasta is al dente, do the taste test – it should feel tender but still with a slight resistance when you chew it.

This method of cooking is called pasta risottata – pasta that you cook like risotto! You throw the raw pasta into the sauce and slowly add water until it's cooked. It gives you a creamier, more velvety sauce. Give it a whirl with spaghetti, capers, garlic and tomatoes and you'll never look back.

Charred Chilli Pepper con Carne

SERVES 4 · TAKES 1 HOUR 15 MINUTES

Despite years of training, my tolerance for spicy food is still feeble at best. There's always an audible sigh whenever I request chilli at my in-laws' house, as they're unable to make their mouth-scalding version that could bring tears to your eyes. Feel free to take this to whatever Scoville level you're comfortable with, but ultimately enjoy the deep, rich flavour of this pepper-laden chilli.

1 tsp olive oil

1 red onion, halved and sliced into half-moons

3 garlic cloves, finely sliced

6 sun-dried tomatoes, finely chopped

2 tsp ground cumin

2 tsp ground paprika

1½ tsp ground coriander

2 tsp chilli powder

400g (14oz) lean minced (ground) meat
    (I like half-and-half turkey and pork)

2 x 400g (14oz) cans of plum tomatoes

1 beef stock cube

1 shot of espresso (or use 2 tsp instant coffee
    granules dissolved in 2 tbsp water)

3 red (bell) peppers, halved and deseeded

2 x 400g (14oz) cans of beans of your choice,
    drained and rinsed (I love a combination
    of kidney and borlotti beans)

Salt

FOR THE GRAINS

200ml (7fl oz/scant 1 cup) chicken stock

100g (3½oz) brown rice

100g (3½oz) quinoa

TO SERVE (OPTIONAL)

Plain yogurt

Lime wedges

Coriander (cilantro) leaves

Heat the oil in a large saucepan or wide-based, deep-sided frying pan over a medium heat, add the red onion and a pinch of salt and cook until softened and turning slightly golden, about 10 minutes. Add the garlic, sun-dried tomatoes and all the spices, then cook for 2–3 minutes more until the fragrances release. Tip the contents of the pan into a bowl and set aside, then put the pan back on the heat.

Add the minced meat to the pan (you may need another small splash of oil) and cook over a high heat, breaking it up as it cooks. When the meat has a gorgeous golden hue, add your onion mixture back to the pan.

Add the plum tomatoes to the pan, giving them a good squeeze as you add them in. Then fill one of the cans with water and add that, too. Crumble in the beef stock cube and pour in the espresso. Give it all a good stir before popping a lid on and bringing it to the boil, then drop to a simmer and cook for 30–35 minutes.

While the meat is cooking, pop the peppers, skin side up, under a very hot grill (broiler) and leave for 10–15 minutes or until the skins have blackened and blistered. When cool enough to handle, peel off the blackened skin and slice the flesh into strips.

Take the lid off your chilli, add the beans and cook for a further 10 minutes. Finally, add your charred red peppers and cook until the sauce is thick and glossy.

Recipe continues overleaf.

COMFORTING CLASSICS

Meanwhile, bring the stock for the grains to a boil in a pan, then add the rice and quinoa. Stir well, then cover and reduce to a simmer for 25 minutes. Keep an eye on it and top up with water if needed. When cooked through and the liquid has disappeared, fluff the grains up with a fork.

Serve the chilli in bowls with the grains. I like to top mine with a drizzle of yogurt, a squeeze of lime and some coriander.

NOTES

If you can bear to wait, this is the best kind of prep-ahead meal. If you cook it, cool it, and refrigerate it (or better yet freeze it), your chilli will thicken as the beans absorb excess liquid, the acidity of the tomatoes will mellow, and the spices and richness of your chilli will deepen.

Red bell peppers are the most nutrient-dense, which makes them the healthiest pepper. This is because they've been on the vine for longer compared with orange, yellow and green peppers.

Minced turkey is a healthier alternative to beef, pork or lamb here. If using minced beef or lamb, opt for 'lean' or, ideally, 'extra lean'.

When you cook your meat, use unsaturated fats (such as olive, rapeseed/canola or sunflower) so you're not adding back the saturated fat you've avoided.

I love to serve my chilli with a simple green salad – a combination of Cos and baby gem work beautifully to cool down those spicy flavours and retain some crunch.

Beef and Mushroom Stroganoff with Spinach Pasta

SERVES 4 · TAKES 1 HOUR

Tender slices of rump steak cooked perfectly pink and dripping in the sauciest of gravies. Creamy, with a bite of pepper and a subtle flare of brandy that nips my nostrils as I inhale every mouthful, fearful I won't finish first and that the 'seconds' will be made that much smaller as my brother eyes up the longest strip of steak still left in the pan. Mum nods to me. A reassurance that that final piece is mine, not just because it's my favourite, but because it's my birthday. Despite decades of beef stroganoffs, this is the dish of choice when it comes to my birthday. My spin on this dish is spinach pasta – something first taught to me by my hero, Jamie Oliver (that man is a genius!).

FOR THE BEEF STROGANOFF
500g (1lb 2oz) bavette (skirt or flank) steak
1 tsp paprika
1 tsp ground black pepper
Small splash of olive oil
1 red onion, finely chopped
Pinch of salt
2 garlic cloves, crushed
400g (14oz) mixed mushrooms, torn
1 tbsp wholegrain mustard
2 tbsp tomato paste
1 beef stock cube
1 tbsp cornflour (cornstarch) mixed
    with 2 tbsp water to form a slurry
150ml (5fl oz/scant ⅔ cup) water
150ml (5fl oz/scant ⅔ cup) sour cream
Handful of flat-leaf parsley, finely chopped

FOR THE SPINACH PASTA
200g (7oz) spinach
Small handful of parsley leaves
280g (10oz) 00 pasta flour
Pinch of salt

Start by making the pasta. Add the ingredients to a food processor and blitz into a dough. Trust the process: it will eventually turn from a crumb into a smooth, tacky pasta dough.

Next, roll the pasta out on a sheet of baking paper dusted with flour, until it is the thickness of a pound coin (about ⅛in). Cover with cling film (plastic wrap) and place it in the fridge while you prepare the stroganoff.

First tenderize your steak. I've chosen bavette steak because it's cheap, lean and full of flavour, but as a cheaper cut it requires a little more TLC. Lay it between 2 pieces of baking paper and give it a bash with the rolling pin. We're not aiming to flatten it too considerably but rather soften it.

Mix together your paprika and pepper, then use it to rub the bashed steak generously on both sides.

Heat a wide-based, deep-sided frying pan over a medium–high heat with the splash of olive oil. Cook your steak for 1–3 minutes on each side, depending on its thickness. Remove from the pan, loosely cover with foil and leave to rest. Set the pan back on the heat.

Add the onion and salt with a splash of water to the pan and cook for 12–15 minutes until soft. Add the garlic and cook for 1–2 minutes until fragrant, then tip the contents of the pan into a bowl and set aside.

Increase the heat under your pan and add your mushrooms. You may need a touch more oil at this point, but we want to see the mushrooms catch colour, not sweat, so don't overcrowd the pan.

Recipe continues overleaf.

Once all your mushrooms have cooked, drop the temperature back down to medium and add back your onions and garlic along with the mustard, tomato paste, beef stock cube and cornflour slurry. Give everything a good stir and cook for 2–3 minutes before adding the water and sour cream. Stir well and cook for 5 more minutes.

Bring a pan of salted water to the boil and remove the pasta sheet from the fridge. Use a pair of scissors to cut off even little 'worms' of pasta, allowing them to drop straight into the boiling water. Cook for about 5 minutes (at which point all the pasta should be floating on the surface), then drain.

While the pasta is cooking, slice your steak into strips, going against the grain so you break the fibres and avoid a chewy steak. Add the steak to the creamy sauce along with any of its juices, then add the parsley and give the stroganoff a good stir. Serve immediately (so you don't overcook your delicious steak) with the spinach pasta.

NOTES

You can use any steak you fancy for this recipe, or leave it out altogether and just amp up the mushroom content to make it veggie-friendly.

A cornflour slurry is a great little kitchen hack to help make sauces thick and glossy without adding too many 'unhealthy' ingredients. It also helps to stabilize ingredients like sour cream and crème fraîche, preventing them from curdling when heated.

COMFORTING CLASSICS

Spiced Carrot and Beetroot Imposter Pie

SERVES 4 · TAKES 1 HOUR

I think it's important to acknowledge when you can't be authentic, and though some of you may not have given it a second thought, my husband will be screaming that pies are only pies if they are completely enveloped in pastry. So, I guess we can call this an imposter pie! Whatever you call it, it's delicious.

500g (1lb 2oz) ready-to-eat cooked beetroot (beet), cut into 2cm (¾in) chunks
2 large carrots, cut into 2cm (¾in) chunks
4 tbsp harissa
½ tsp ground cinnamon
1 tsp salt
100g (3½oz) spinach
200ml (7fl oz/scant 1 cup) hot vegetable stock
80g (2¾oz) feta, crumbled
4 tbsp reduced-fat crème fraîche
6 sheets of filo (phyllo) pastry
1 tbsp butter, melted

Preheat the oven to 220°C (200°C fan/425°F/gas 7).

Put the beetroot and carrots on a lined baking tray and rub with the harissa, cinnamon and salt. Bake in the oven for 20–22 minutes (turning halfway through) until tender and slightly crisped.

Reduce the oven temperature to 160°C (140°C fan/325°F/gas 3).

Add the spinach to a bowl and pour over the hot vegetable stock so the spinach starts to wilt. Add your roasted veggies, crumbled feta and crème fraîche to the bowl and stir until well combined. Pour the filling into a pie tin or dish.

Scrunch up each filo sheet into a little rosette and pop on top of the pie filling to cover it. Brush with the melted butter and bake for 20–25 minutes until the pastry is golden. Serve and enjoy!

Chicken and Tarragon Pot Pie with a Herby Polenta Lid

SERVES 4 · TAKES 1 HOUR 15 MINUTES

One of the great satisfactions of pie is that first slice. The clean cut of the crust, the steam wafting into the air carrying the tantalizing scent of what's inside, the perfect triangle lifted onto the plate, stoically holding shape until it topples sideways the moment you attack it with your knife and fork.

FOR THE HERBY POLENTA LID

250ml (9fl oz/1 cup) hot vegetable stock
75g (2½oz) polenta (fine cornmeal)
1 large free-range egg, beaten, plus extra
    for the egg wash
Handful of chopped parsley

FOR THE FILLING

1 tbsp olive oil
2 boneless, skinless chicken breasts,
    cut into 2cm (¾in) chunks
1 tbsp plain (all-purpose) flour
1 leek, finely sliced
150g (5½oz) mushrooms, finely sliced
Good pinch of salt
2 tsp dried tarragon or ½ bunch of fresh
    tarragon, finely chopped
1 tsp Dijon mustard
4 tbsp reduced-fat crème fraîche
About 200ml (7fl oz/scant 1 cup) vegetable stock

Preheat the oven to 220°C (200°C fan/425°F/gas 7).

Place the stock in a pan set over a low–medium heat. Once hot, pour in the polenta while stirring continuously. Once combined, lower the heat, cover and stir every 5 minutes or so for 15–20 minutes until the stock has been absorbed and the polenta has thickened. Remove from the heat and beat in the egg and parsley.

Pour the polenta mixture onto a lined and greased baking tray, then shape it to the same dimensions of your chosen pie dish (I use a shallow casserole pan), to create your pie lid. Brush the polenta with egg wash and bake in the oven for 15 minutes.

While that is cooking, make your filling. Heat the oil in a shallow casserole pan set over a high heat, add the chicken and cook until crisping and turning golden. Sprinkle over the flour, making sure it's well distributed, then stir well so the chicken is coated.

Add the leek, mushrooms and salt to the pan, then drop the temperature a little and cook and sweat the veggies until they begin to soften (if using dried tarragon, add that now). Stir in the mustard and the crème fraîche, then pour in the stock little by little, until you have a thick and generous sauce. Allow everything to come up to a simmer (if using fresh tarragon, add it now) for a couple of minutes, then remove the pan from the heat.

Carefully invert your baked polenta lid on top of the pie filling (so it is now upside down with the glazed side face-down). Brush the topside of the polenta with egg wash, then place the pan into the oven for 30 minutes, until the pie is golden and bubbling.

NOTES

Fresh tarragon should be used raw or added towards the end of cooking; if left to cook a long time, the flavour will turn bitter. Dried tarragon is added early on in recipes but will not create the same effect as fresh, due to its diminished flavour.

Beef Stew with Giant Squash Gnocchi Dumplings

SERVES 6 · TAKES 3 HOURS 30 MINUTES

On bonfire night, our annual tradition is packing up a Thermos of stew, a Tupperware of dumplings, a vat of tea and a blanket to go and watch the local fireworks. The ratio of dumplings to stew is alarmingly even, and despite me feigning 'no, you have it' at least three times, I will always be given the last dumpling. Food is my love language, and my wonderful husband speaks it fluently.

1 tbsp olive oil

700g (1½lb) lean beef braising steak, cut into 5cm (2in) cubes

2 tbsp plain (all-purpose) flour, seasoned with salt and pepper

2 brown onions, each cut into eighths

2 celery sticks, thinly sliced

2 carrots, unpeeled, cut into 2cm (¾in) chunks

1 parsnip, unpeeled, cut into 2cm (¾in) chunks

1 x 400g (14oz) can of plum tomatoes

2 beef stock cubes

2 tsp dried thyme

3 bay leaves

4 tbsp apple cider vinegar

1 heaped tbsp Dijon mustard

Salt and ground black pepper

FOR THE GNOCCHI DUMPLINGS

700g (1½lb) sweet potatoes (about 4 medium sweet potatoes)

400g (14oz) self-raising flour

1 tsp salt

1 tsp dried thyme

Preheat the oven to 200°C (180°C fan/400°F/gas 6).

Heat the oil in a large casserole pan. Roll your beef in the seasoned flour, then add to the pan (ensuring it isn't piled up as we want the beef to get a golden crust, not stew at this point). Brown it on all sides.

Add the onions, celery, carrots and parsnips. Chuck in any leftover seasoned flour and fry for 2–3 minutes.

Add the tomatoes, giving them a good squeeze as you add them, then fill the can with water and add that too. Repeat with another canful of water. Add the stock cubes, thyme and bay leaves and season generously, then give it all a stir – scrape the bottom of the pan to loosen any crispy bits. Cover the pan with a lid and pop it in the oven for 2 hours.

Meanwhile, make the gnocchi dumplings. Bake the sweet potatoes whole alongside the stew, for 45–50 minutes, or until soft. Allow to cool for at least 30 minutes, so they are cool enough to handle, then remove the skin and mash the flesh. Add the flour, salt and thyme and knead to form a dough (this is best done with the help of a dough scraper or wooden spoon, as the dough is quite sticky – trust the process!). Wet your hands and divide the dough into 8 balls.

When the stew has had its 2 hours, remove the lid and stir through the cider vinegar and mustard. Pop your dumplings, evenly spaced, on the surface of the stew, then place the lid back on and cook in the oven for a further 1 hour until the dumplings are plump and the stew has thickened.

Spiced Chicken and Loaded Veggie Traybake

SERVES 4 · TAKES 1 HOUR 35 MINUTES

Traybakes were the food of my twenties. Never having a dishwasher while living in a house share meant a frequent lack of clean equipment, paired with even less desire to wash up – a vicious circle. This juicy spiced chicken is buried in a medley of rich roasted veggies, with vibrant pops of peas and chickpeas and lashings of yogurt to keep you fuller for longer.

8 chicken drumsticks
2 tbsp olive oil
4 garlic cloves, crushed
Thumb-sized piece of fresh ginger, grated
1 tbsp garam masala
2 tsp cumin seeds
1 tsp ground turmeric
3 heaped tbsp low-fat plain yogurt
200g (7oz) new potatoes, halved
200g (7oz) cherry tomatoes
2 red onions, peeled and quartered
1 x 400g (14oz) can of chickpeas, drained
    and rinsed
1 x 400g (14oz) can of plum tomatoes
150g (5½oz) thawed frozen peas
Salt and ground black pepper

TO SERVE
Sliced green chilli
Coriander (cilantro) leaves
Low-fat plain yogurt

Add the chicken drumsticks to a large bowl with 1 tablespoon of the oil, the garlic, ginger, garam masala, cumin seeds, turmeric and yogurt. Toss together with your hands until coated. Leave to marinate for at least 30 minutes (or in the fridge overnight).

Preheat the oven to 200°C (180°C fan/400°F/gas 6).

Put the potatoes, cherry tomatoes, onions, chickpeas and canned tomatoes in a large roasting tin. Add the remaining tablespoon of oil and plenty of salt and pepper, then toss everything together. Bury the chicken drumsticks (along with any remaining yogurt marinade) in between the veggies, then bake for 1 hour until cooked and golden.

Add the peas to the roasting tin and return to the oven for a further 5 minutes.

Serve scattered with green chilli and coriander, with dollops of yogurt.

The Veggie Table

I couldn't write this book without including the recipe that brought me here in the first place: Grandma's leek and potato soup. Basic ingredients, cooked with a whole load of love and zero fuss.

We all know that vegetables are good for us, but we do have an exceptional ability to turn the very good into the very bad (yes, Grandma, I'm talking about the block of butter and pint of cream you used to add to your soup!). So this chapter is all about elevating your veggies with some simple techniques, to make them as delicious as they are good for you.

Sweet Potato Hash Sunny Side Up

SERVES 4 · TAKES 30 MINUTES

Some of our most used recipes are born from a fridge clear out. The days when we have no intention of leaving the house and heading to the shops, but want to eat something indulgent and delicious. My husband has an unmatched ability to open the cupboard and see hope beyond the sprouting potato and can of beans, and this is one of those dishes.

3 tbsp olive oil

1 x 400g (14oz) can of butterbeans (lima beans), drained, rinsed and dried thoroughly with some kitchen paper

1 red onion, halved and thinly sliced into half-moons

6 sprigs of thyme

1–2 red chillies (go with your heat preference), deseeded and thinly sliced

2 tbsp water

300g (10½oz) sweet potato, unpeeled and cubed

300g (10½oz) butternut squash, unpeeled, deseeded and cubed

1 fried free-range egg per serving

Salt and ground black pepper

Add 1 tablespoon of the oil to a large frying pan and add your butterbeans. Cook and stir until lightly golden and crispy. Transfer from the pan into a bowl and set aside. Pop the pan back on the heat.

Add the onion, thyme and chillies to the pan with another tablespoon of oil and the water. Cook for 5–7 minutes, stirring occasionally, so the onions sweat and soften (but do not colour). Remove from the pan to the same bowl as the butterbeans.

Add the remaining oil to the pan along with the sweet potato and butternut squash, then turn up the heat to medium–high. Generously add some salt and black pepper, then stir to coat. Cover the pan and cook for 10–15 minutes, lifting the lid every 5 minutes or so to flip and stir the vegetables. They should be golden and soft by the time they're cooked.

Tip the butterbeans and onions back into the pan and stir to combine everything, then remove from the heat. Serve topped with fried eggs.

FRIED EGG DICTIONARY

Sunny side up – is when you can see the bright yellow yolk on top and it's beautifully runny. The egg is cracked into the pan and cooked continuously on one side.

Over easy – means the egg is flipped during cooking so there's no visible sunny yolk but the yolk is still quite runny.

Over medium – the egg is flipped and cooked a little longer, so the yolk has that 'almost-set' quality.

Over hard – flipped and the yolk is firm.

THE VEGGIE TABLE

THE VEGGIE TABLE

Clever Corn Ribs 3 Ways

SERVES 4 · TAKES 20–35 MINUTES

I vividly remember the first corn on the cob I truly appreciated. It wasn't even that long ago, and it was from a road-side grocer in Canada. I ate it raw, and it was mind-blowingly sweet. We bought some more of these golden husks then sliced them up into 'ribs' and roasted them on the BBQ on the bank of a river, with all manner of seasonings. Good times! I've given you three variations here, so simply select whichever one you fancy.

4 corn cobs, husks removed

FOR THE CLASSIC
2 tbsp olive oil
1 tsp paprika
2 tsp garlic granules
1 tsp onion granules
To serve: chopped spring onion (scallion), chopped red chillies and a dollop of reduced-fat crème fraîche

FOR THE THAI GREEN
1 tbsp olive oil
2 tbsp Thai green chilli paste (shop-bought; check it's vegetarian, if needed)
2 tbsp coconut cream
To serve: coriander (cilantro) and a squeeze of lime

FOR THE MISO
2 tbsp white miso
2 tbsp olive oil
2 tsp Tabasco sauce
2 tsp white wine vinegar
2 tsp honey
To serve: finely chopped mint

Firstly, make your chosen spice rub or paste by simply combining all the ingredients from your chosen 'style' of corn rib.

Slice your corn cobs lengthways into quarters. Please be careful – the best way to do this is to stand the cob on its end and slice from the top downwards, using a gentle rocking motion. In a large bowl, drench the corn in your chosen rub or paste, ensuring the corn is completely coated.

To cook in the oven, preheat the oven to 220°C (200°C fan/425°F/gas 7). Spread your seasoned corn ribs in a single layer on a lined baking tray and roast for 20–25 minutes. You won't get as big a 'curl' on them when oven roasting, but they will be totally delicious.

To air-fry, heat the air-fryer to 180°C/350°F and cook for 12–15 minutes, turning them halfway.

NOTES

I highly recommend having miso paste in your pantry because it is so versatile. It can be used in a variety of dishes, including soups, stews, marinades, dressings and even desserts. It adds depth and complexity to dishes and can be used as a substitute for other salty or savoury ingredients such as soy sauce or salt.

Saucy Caesar Salad Cups
with Crunchy Tofu Croutons

SERVES 4 · TAKES 30 MINUTES

My first 'proper' job – excluding the café at a children's activity centre where I truly refined my cheese-sandwich-making skills – was at a health spa. Every now and then I would 'accidentally' forget my packed lunch and be forced into heading to the spa restaurant where the Caesar salad would make me feel as classy as the customers. This dish is something we always sneakily pop on the 'healthy list', but with this dressing, it really is!

280g (10oz) extra-firm tofu, sliced into 1cm (½in) cubes
1 tbsp cornflour (cornstarch)
1 tbsp olive oil
1 vegetable stock cube, crushed
¼ tsp ground white pepper
¼ tsp garlic granules
1 romaine or 2 baby gem lettuce
4 free-range eggs, boiled to your preference (see overleaf)
40g (1½oz) vegetarian hard cheese, shaved
40g (1½oz) pumpkin seeds (optional)

FOR THE DRESSING
1 small garlic clove
100g (3½oz) low-fat plain yogurt
Drizzle of olive oil
2 tsp white miso

Preheat the oven to 220°C (200°C fan/425°F/gas 7).

For the dressing, crush your garlic clove – try finely slicing and then smashing the pieces into your chopping board using long strokes with the flat side of your knife to make a fine paste. Add to a small bowl or jug (pitcher) with the yogurt, olive oil and miso, then whisk until smooth. Your dressing is done!

Tofu is high in protein and a great carrier of flavour. We're going to bake our tofu to add a crispy bite to our salad cups. Gently press the tofu cubes in a clean tea (dish) towel to remove excess moisture.

In a bowl, mix the cornflour, olive oil, crushed stock cube, white pepper and garlic granules. Toss and evenly coat your tofu cubes in the paste, then spread in a single layer on a baking tray. Bake in the oven for 15–20 minutes until golden.

Let's assemble your salad. Separate the lettuce leaves and lay on a plate. Spoon some dressing into the cup of each leaf and then sprinkle over some tofu cubes. Quarter your boiled eggs and add these too, then sprinkle over some cheese shavings and pumpkin seeds, if using. Drizzle with any extra dressing, if you like, then serve.

NOTES

If you don't need to make this vegetarian, try replacing the miso in the dressing for 2 crushed anchovies packed in oil.

THE VEGGIE TABLE

. a guide to .

Boiling Eggs

Here is my foolproof guide to boiling eggs like a pro.

Use free-range eggs and cook them from room temperature, gently lowering them into boiling water. I like to pierce a small hole on the widest end of the egg (or use an egg pricker).

SOFT-BOILED

A set white and a runny yolk (the ideal dippy egg)

3 minutes – medium egg

4 minutes – large egg

5 minutes – extra-large egg

MEDIUM-BOILED (KNOWN AS 'MOLLET')

A firmer but sticky yolk that has a little bit of runniness to it and a firm white.

4 minutes – medium egg

5 minutes – large egg

6 minutes – extra-large egg

HARD-BOILED

Firm whites and yolks, these are smashable for an egg mayo but won't be crumbly and dry.

7 minutes – medium egg

8 minutes – large egg

9 minutes – extra-large egg

Purple Potato Salad

SERVES 4 · TAKES 30 MINUTES

Potato salad means summer to me. It's spreading old blankets across the morning dew as the day begins to warm up. It's nestling bottles of booze into buckets filled with water and ice while everyone brings a dish. It's making up garden games and decanting all the leftovers back into Tupperware to be eaten the whole week long.

600g (1lb 5oz) new potatoes, halved
1 tbsp light olive oil or vegetable oil
200g (7oz) ready-to-eat cooked beetroot
130g (4¾oz) 0% fat Greek yogurt
Juice of 1 lemon
60g (2¼oz) feta
2 tbsp capers
1 large shallot, finely chopped
Large handful of parsley, roughly chopped
Small handful of mint, roughly chopped
Salt

Boil the new potatoes in a large pot of salted water for 15–20 minutes until tender, then drain and allow to cool.

Set a large frying pan over a medium–high heat and add the oil. In batches – we just want a single layer each time – add your potatoes to the hot pan. With a masher or a fork, apply pressure to the top of each potato so they pop and crush into a slightly flattened spud that's still holding together. Cook for 3–4 minutes before flipping each one and cooking the other side for a further 3–4 minutes. We want them to crisp not steam – these potatoes will add a lovely crunch to your potato salad (fry for longer if you want them to be super-crispy and crunchy). Transfer the potatoes to a serving dish.

Add the beetroot, yogurt, lemon juice and feta to a blender and whizz until smooth. Pour this over your potatoes, then add the capers, shallot, parsley and mint.

Toss everything well, then serve.

NOTES

Waxy potatoes like Charlotte, Jersey Royals or any new potatoes are best for potato salad – they hold together better during the boiling process and don't fall apart when tossed. Try to avoid using floury potatoes, as these are more likely to crumble.

Your prepared salad will store in the fridge for up to 3 days until you're ready to tuck in, or it can be frozen in an airtight container for up to 3 months.

THE VEGGIE TABLE

THE VEGGIE TABLE

Super Green Salad

SERVES 4 · TAKES 10 MINUTES

Comfort food doesn't always mean butter and sugar. Whenever I get home after a holiday or a weekend of heavy socializing, I take great comfort in recharging my body with good things that feel nourishing. But salads needn't ever be bland or unsatisfying...

1 cucumber
½ white cabbage, very finely sliced
3 spring onions (scallions), finely sliced
½ bunch of chives (10g/⅓oz), finely chopped

FOR THE DRESSING
1½ tbsp extra virgin olive oil
½ tbsp white wine vinegar
Juice of 1 lemon
½ tsp salt
60g (2¼oz) cashews
3 tbsp cottage cheese
1 shallot, peeled
1 garlic clove, peeled
½ bunch of basil (15g/½oz), stalks and leaves
Large handful of spinach
30g (1oz) Parmesan

Halve the cucumber lengthways, use a teaspoon to scrape out the seeds, then dice it. Add to a bowl with the cabbage, spring onions and chives.

Put all the dressing ingredients in a blender or food processor and blend until lovely and smooth. If the dressing seems a little thick, you can loosen it with up to 2 tablespoons of water. Pour the dressing into the bowl of veg, mix until really well coated, then serve.

Pictured on the right.

Pickled Slaw Tabbouleh

SERVES 4 · TAKES 25 MINUTES

This dish is a celebration of flavour – firing your senses with sweet, salty, sour and bitter notes, all balanced perfectly. Learning styles of dishes like tabbouleh is such an easy gateway into being creative with food. I seriously urge you to book a meal somewhere you've never eaten before, with a cuisine you're less familiar with, and it will surprise you how inspiring an experience it can be.

100g (3½oz) bulgur wheat

200g (7oz) radishes, thinly sliced

1 carrot, julienned (or coarsely grated if you don't have the time or patience; see Notes)

1 red onion, halved and thinly sliced into half-moons

¼ white cabbage, very finely sliced

3 tbsp white wine vinegar

Juice of 1 lemon

1 Pink Lady apple, cored and diced

Handful of mint leaves, roughly chopped

Large handful of parsley leaves, roughly chopped

Large handful coriander (cilantro) leaves, roughly chopped

40g (1½oz) shelled pistachios, roughly chopped

2 tbsp extra virgin olive oil

Salt

Put the bulgur wheat into a heatproof bowl and pour over a kettle of boiling water, so the water comes about 2–3cm (¾–1¼in) above the grains. Cover the bowl with a plate or tea (dish) towel and leave to soak for 20 minutes until all the water is absorbed (you can use boiling stock instead of water, if you like, for more flavour).

Meanwhile, put your prepared radishes, carrot, red onion and cabbage in a bowl and mix. Add the vinegar, half the lemon juice and a pinch of salt. Give everything a mix and a scrunch with your hands then leave to sit for 10–15 minutes.

Toss your apple into the pickled vegetables, then give everything a good squeeze to remove excess moisture, pouring it away.

Drain the bulgur (if necessary) and combine it with the vegetables. Mix in the herbs, pistachios, the remaining lemon juice and the olive oil, then taste and season with salt, if needed, before serving.

Pictured on page 82.

NOTES

'To julienne' is to cut your food into short, thin strips – like matchsticks. Some mandolines have a julienne blade, which makes things easier and quicker. However, you can also use a coarse grater to get a similar effect.

Save your herb stalks (they freeze well) for adding to pestos, soups and broths, or the pea and avocado salsa verde (opposite).

. pick me up .

Awesome Avocado Dips 3 Ways

SERVES 4 · TAKES 10 MINUTES

Unsurprisingly, when I worked at Jamie Oliver's, the staff kitchens were always well supplied, most notably with avocados. Balancing my pay cheque and London rent meant I wouldn't dare miss out on these expensive freebies. The only problem – I didn't like avocado. Never one to be defeated by taste, I persisted and worked it into several dishes until I realized the avocado was all I ever needed in the first place.

AVOCADO AND CITRUS SALSA

1 large orange, segmented and diced
1 grapefruit, segmented and diced
1 ripe avocado, peeled, pitted and cubed
1 red chilli, finely chopped
½ bunch of coriander (cilantro), finely chopped
Juice of 1 lime
Salt and ground black pepper

CREAMY AVOCADO DIP

Bunch of spring onions (scallions), trimmed
1 tbsp olive oil
120g (4¼oz) low-fat plain yogurt
2 ripe avocados, peeled and pitted
Juice of 1 lime
Salt and ground black pepper, to taste

PEA AND AVOCADO SALSA VERDE

1 ripe avocado, peeled and pitted
150g (5½oz) frozen peas, thawed
1–2 garlic cloves, crushed
1 tbsp white wine vinegar
Pinch of sugar
Bunch of parsley, finely chopped
½ bunch of basil, finely chopped
Handful of mint leaves, finely chopped
1 tbsp capers
1 tbsp roughly chopped gherkins
Salt and ground black pepper, to taste

For the avocado and citrus salsa: throw everything into a bowl with salt and pepper to taste, and mix well.

For the creamy avocado dip: rub the spring onions with the olive oil and a pinch of salt and pan-fry for 10 minutes over a gentle heat until golden and soft. Throw your yogurt, avocados, lime juice and half the spring onions into a blender and whizz until smooth. Season with salt and pepper and serve with your remaining spring onions, chopped, on top.

For the pea and avocado salsa verde: add the avocado, peas, garlic, vinegar and sugar to a blender and blitz until smooth. Fold in the herbs, capers and gherkins and taste for seasoning.

NOTES

Segment your orange and grapefruit by using a sharp knife to cut off the top and bottom. Use even downward strokes to slice the skin away from the flesh, getting rid of the white pith. Cut between the membranes to segment it.

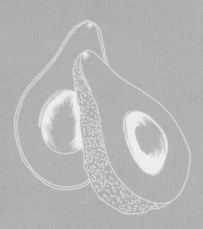

THE VEGGIE TABLE

Leek, Pea and Potato Soup with Buttery Cornbread

SERVES 4 · TAKES 40 MINUTES

In a Liverpool kitchen not altered since the early '80s, Grandma digs out her trusted saucepan and clicks on the temperamental stove. Me and my brother have slept during the 4½-hour journey and are recharged, while Mum and Dad nurse a hot cup of tea and shake off the stress of the M1. We eagerly await the ladles of rich leek and potato soup – it engulfs us with a warm hug and we dip in hunks of crusty white bread spread with an inch-thick slab of butter. It turns out the secret to her legendary soup is a metric ton of butter. And yes, it nourished our souls, but here's a version that nourishes our bodies, too.

FOR THE CORNBREAD

Oil or softened butter, for greasing
140g (5oz) wholemeal (wholewheat) flour
100g (3½oz) polenta (fine cornmeal)
3 tsp baking powder
¼ tsp fine salt
250ml (9fl oz/1 cup) skimmed milk
    (or dairy-free alternative)
30g (1oz) butter, melted
2 tbsp runny honey
1 medium free-range egg, lightly beaten

FOR THE SOUP

2 tbsp olive oil
4 large leeks, finely sliced
1 brown onion, finely chopped
2 garlic cloves, crushed
2 large red potatoes (about 450g/1lb), unpeeled
    and cut into 3cm (1¼in) cubes
½ head cauliflower (about 400g/14oz),
    cut into small florets
1.2l (40fl oz/5 cups) vegetable stock
200g (7oz) frozen peas
2 tbsp reduced-fat crème fraîche or sour cream
1 tsp lemon juice
Salt and ground black pepper

For the cornbread, preheat the oven to 210°C (190°C fan/410°F/gas 6–7). Grease a 20cm (8in) springform cake tin (pan) with a light layer of oil or softened butter and line with baking paper.

In a medium bowl, mix the flour, polenta, baking powder and salt. Make a well in the middle of the dry ingredients and pour in the milk, melted butter, honey and egg. Stir into a smooth batter.

Scrape the batter into the cake tin and bake for 20–25 minutes until a skewer poked into the centre comes out clean. Set aside until ready to serve (let the cornbread cool for 10 minutes before slicing).

Meanwhile, for the soup, place a large pot over a medium heat and add the olive oil, leeks, onion and a pinch of salt, stirring to coat with oil. Pop on the lid, turn the heat to low and sweat for 8–10 minutes until soft. Remove the lid, stir in the garlic and cook for a few minutes more so the vegetables catch a light tinge of golden colour.

Add the potatoes, cauliflower and stock, bring to the boil over a high heat, then reduce to a light simmer for 15 minutes, or until the cauliflower and potatoes are tender. Add the peas and cook for a further 2–4 minutes.

Using a hand blender (or food processor or blender) blitz your soup until smooth. Add the crème fraîche, lemon juice and a generous amount of freshly ground black pepper, then blend again. Taste and season with salt, if needed.

Ladle the soup into bowls and serve with wedges of warm cornbread alongside.

NOTES

The soup will keep in an airtight container for up to 3 days in the fridge, or 3 months in the freezer.

Store the cornbread wrapped tightly in a cool, dry place for up to 3 days. If wrapped securely it will last up to 10 days in the fridge, or 3 months in the freezer.

THE VEGGIE TABLE

Chunky Minestrone Soup with Garlic Breadsticks

SERVES 4 · TAKES 1 HOUR

When my husband and I moved into our first home together, I was convinced I would have a perfectly labelled pantry and live by a weekly meal planner – but I am not that person. Minestrone masks my lack of organization by forcing me into preparing large vats of soup using store-cupboard essentials and my growing collection of expiring vegetables. Raid your vegetable drawer and do the same!

1 tbsp olive oil, plus extra for greasing

1 brown onion, chopped

1 carrot, unpeeled, chopped

1 celery stick, chopped

3 parsley stems, finely chopped

2 rosemary sprigs (leaves only), finely chopped

1 bay leaf

1 x 400g (14oz) can of plum tomatoes

1 x 400g (14oz) can of borlotti beans or chickpeas, drained and rinsed

1.2l (40fl oz/5 cups) vegetable stock

100g (3½oz) wholewheat pasta (shape of your choice)

250–350g (9–12oz) mixed greens (kale, spinach, chard, bok choy, cabbage, spring greens)

Salt

FOR THE EASY GARLIC BREADSTICKS

140ml (4¾fl oz/generous ½ cup) warm water

3g (1 tsp) fast-action dried yeast

Pinch of granulated sugar

100g (3½oz) wholemeal (wholewheat) flour

110g (3¾oz) plain (all-purpose) flour

½ tsp salt

20g (¾oz) salted butter

2 garlic cloves, crushed

2 tbsp finely chopped parsley leaves

For the breadsticks, combine the warm water with the yeast and sugar in a large bowl and let sit until little frothy bubbles form on the surface. Add the flours and salt and mix until it forms a smooth dough. Knead for 2–3 minutes until smooth, then place back into the bowl, cover with a clean tea (dish) towel, and leave somewhere warm (see Note overleaf) to prove for 15 minutes.

Tip the dough out onto a lightly oiled baking tray, pat it out into a rectangle roughly 15 x 20cm (6 x 8in) and score deeply (but not all the way through) into 8 long breadsticks. Cover and let rise for 15 minutes somewhere warm while you preheat the oven to 210°C (190°C fan/410°F/gas 6–7).

Meanwhile, make the garlic butter by combining the butter and garlic in a small pan or frying pan. Cook over a medium heat until the butter is fully melted and the garlic is fragrant. Remove from the heat and stir in the parsley.

Uncover the risen breadsticks and bake as a whole for 15–20 minutes until turning brown around the edges. Brush with the garlic butter while still warm then tear and share.

For the soup, heat the oil in a large pot over a medium–low heat, add the onion, carrot, celery and a little salt and sauté for 7–10 minutes until softened. Add the fresh herbs and the tomatoes, mashing them lightly with the back of your spoon.

Stir in the beans and vegetable stock, bring to the boil, then turn down to a simmer and cover with a lid. Allow everything to simmer merrily for 20–25 minutes. Uncover and stir in the pasta. Five minutes before the pasta is fully cooked (check the back of the packet for the cooking time), add the greens and leave to simmer until the pasta is cooked through and the greens are soft.

Taste for seasoning, remove and discard the bay leaf, and serve the soup with your beautiful breadsticks.

Recipe continues overleaf.

NOTES

For proving bread, one of the best places for
it to stay warm is a switched-off oven! I preheat
the oven to 50°C (120°F/gas lowest setting) for
2 minutes, then switch it off completely. Place
a folded tea (dish) towel in the bottom of the oven
(this protects the bottom of the bowl from getting
too hot from touching the metal) and place the
covered bowl inside with the door shut. This
keeps the dough toasty. Just make sure you stick
a note to the oven door so that no one turns it
on by accident while the dough is in there rising.
Another way to create a proving oven is to pour
boiling water into a roasting tray on the bottom
shelf of the oven and place your dough on a shelf
above it. With the oven door kept shut, it will stay
warm and moist for hours.

Whole canned plum tomatoes tend to be less
processed than chopped ones, which means they
have a fresher flavour and keep more of their
natural sweetness.

The soup will keep happily in an airtight container
in the fridge for 3 days or in the freezer for up
to 3 months. To reheat from frozen, make sure
to use medium–low heat and stir it frequently to
stop it catching before it's thawed (you can also
add a couple of tablespoons of water to the pan
while it is thawing).

THE VEGGIE TABLE

Roasted Tomato and Garlic Soup
with Parmesan Crisps

SERVES 4 · TAKES 1 HOUR

Cold Saturday dog walks are always best followed by a hearty bowl of tomato soup. This recipe feels outrageously decadent, with richly roasted tomatoes and fancy Parmesan crisps, but this is simple cooking.

2kg (4lb 6oz) tomatoes, all different shapes, sizes and varieties

2 tbsp olive oil, plus extra for the garlic

Bunch of basil, stalks and leaves separated; stalks finely chopped, leaves left whole

1 whole bulb of garlic

3 tbsp reduced-fat crème fraîche

1 vegetable stock cube, crumbled

1 tsp sugar (optional)

8 tsp grated Parmesan or vegetarian hard cheese (about 10g/⅓oz)

Salt and ground black pepper

NOTES

The soup will keep happily in an airtight container for 3 days in the fridge or in the freezer for up to 3 months. To reheat from frozen, make sure to use medium–low heat and stir it frequently to stop it catching before it's thawed (you can also add a couple of tablespoons of water to the pan while it is thawing).

The Parmesan crisps will keep for 2–3 days in a cool, dry place.

Preheat the oven to 200°C (180°C fan/400°F/gas 6).

Slice the tomatoes into relatively equal sizes, keeping them as large as possible. Toss them with the oil, the chopped basil stalks and some salt and pepper, then tip into a roasting tray.

Slice the very top off the garlic bulb so the cloves are exposed, keeping the rest intact (skins and all). Pop your bulb onto a piece of foil with a bit of olive oil dripped on top and some salt sprinkled over, then close the foil so the garlic bulb is tightly wrapped. Add this to your roasting tray.

Roast in the oven for 40–60 minutes until your tomatoes have started to catch, have shrunk a little and are even bubbling (the time will depend on how much water your tomatoes contain, and their size). Remove from the oven.

Unwrap the garlic and, when cool enough to handle, squeeze out the butter-like cloves into a large pan, discarding the skins. Add the tomatoes to the pan, along with the crème fraîche, vegetable stock cube and half the basil leaves, then use a hand blender to blitz until smooth. Taste and season with salt and the sugar, if needed. Keep warm over a low heat.

For the Parmesan crisps, select your best non-stick frying pan. Place individual teaspoons of grated Parmesan into the dry pan, then set it over a low heat. The cheese should gently melt and cook – you can flatten each pile with a spoon or fish slice to help it crisp. After 2–3 minutes, or until melted and turning golden at the edges, flip each crisp carefully and cook the other side for 1–2 minutes. Transfer to a cool, flat surface (like a plate) and allow to cool and crisp up for a few minutes.

Serve the soup in bowls or mugs with the remaining basil leaves scattered on top and the Parmesan crisps served alongside for scooping, dipping or even crumbling over the soup.

Charred Cabbage and Chips with Punchy Peppercorn Sauce

SERVES 4 · TAKES 1 HOUR 15 MINUTES

There's something about a peppercorn sauce that reminds me of going to a restaurant with my parents and stealing the dregs from my mum's plate to mop up my chips. If a peppercorn sauce is involved, I am licking the plate – and with this version, I can do so whenever I fancy!

1 Savoy or white cabbage
1 tbsp olive oil
½ tsp garlic granules
¼ tsp cayenne pepper
½ tbsp dark soy sauce

FOR THE PEPPERCORN SAUCE
100g (3½oz) cashews
500ml (17fl oz/2 cups) vegetable stock
½ tsp Marmite or 1 tbsp dark soy sauce
1 tbsp olive oil
3 shallots, finely diced
2 tsp black peppercorns, lightly crushed
½ tsp ground white pepper
½ tsp white wine vinegar or lemon juice

FOR THE CHIPS (FRIES)
4 red-skinned potatoes, unpeeled, diced into equal-sized, chunky batons
1 tbsp vegetable or light olive oil
Salt

For the peppercorn sauce, add the cashews, stock and Marmite (or soy sauce) to a small pan. Bring to the boil, then simmer for 10 minutes to soften.

Heat the olive oil in a medium, non-stick frying pan set over a medium heat. Add the shallots and cook for about 7 minutes, stirring often, until turning golden. Add the crushed black peppercorns and ground white pepper and stir for a minute or so to release the fragrance, then remove from the heat.

Tip the contents of the cashew pan into a blender and blitz until smooth. Add the vinegar or lemon juice and blend again until smooth. Pour the creamy cashew liquid into the frying pan with the shallots and stir, loosening with water if needed, to get a pourable, unctuous sauce. Set aside, ready to warm gently before serving.

Preheat the oven to 240°C (220°C fan/475°F/gas 9).

For the chips, drop the potato batons into a pan of boiling, salted water, and boil for 5–7 minutes until tender but not breaking apart. Drain in a colander and leave to steam-dry for at least 10 minutes. Add to a baking tray and rub gently with the oil to coat, then sprinkle with salt. Place in the hot oven.

Meanwhile, slice the cabbage from top to base into slabs 2.5cm (1in) thick, leaving the core intact. Mix together the oil, garlic granules, cayenne pepper and soy sauce, then brush it onto your cabbage slices. Heat a griddle pan over a high heat and add the cabbage. Grill for 5–7 minutes, until starting to char underneath, then flip and cook the other side until starting to blacken, too. Transfer to a baking tray.

Give the chips a good shuffle after they've been in the oven for 15 minutes, then slide the tray of cabbage into the oven. Cook everything for a further 15–20 minutes. The cabbage should be tender and the chips golden and crisp.

Plate up the cabbage with the chips, spooning the warm peppercorn sauce on top, then serve.

Aubergine Bake
with Zingy Tzatziki

Preparing food to be shared is a comfort to me. The action of placing a delicious traybake into the centre of the table and watching the family tuck in is satisfying in itself – especially when I know it not only tastes good, but is good for them too.

2 aubergines (eggplants), cut into 2cm (¾in) chunks

1 tbsp olive oil

2 tbsp harissa

1 tsp ground cinnamon

1 tsp dried oregano

400g (14oz) cherry or baby plum tomatoes

2 red onions, peeled and quartered

1 x 400g (14oz) can of cannellini beans, drained and rinsed

Salt

FOR THE TZATZIKI

½ cucumber, deseeded and cut into 1cm (½in) chunks

150g (5½oz) 0% fat Greek yogurt

1 garlic clove, crushed

Handful of mint leaves, finely chopped

TO SERVE

1 lemon, cut into wedges

Flatbreads (see page 151); optional

Preheat the oven to 220°C (200°C fan/425°F/gas 7).

Place the aubergines in a roasting dish and smother with the oil, harissa, cinnamon, dried oregano and a pinch of salt. Pop in the oven for 15 minutes.

Throw the tomatoes, onions and beans into the aubergine dish and toss to combine. Cover the roasting dish tightly with foil and return to the oven for 15 minutes. Remove the foil, give everything a good stir and bake for a further 25–30 minutes until the veggies are turning golden around the edges.

Make your quick tzatziki by mixing the cucumber, yogurt, garlic and mint together in a small bowl. Season with salt and loosen with a little water (1–2 tablespoons) to create a thick drizzle.

Once your bake is ready, spoon over your tzatziki and dive in, serving lemon wedges on the side for squeezing over, and flatbreads for scooping.

THE VEGGIE TABLE

THE VEGGIE TABLE

Green Vegetable Pasta Bake

SERVES 4 · TAKES 1 HOUR

My Nanny told me my hair would go curly if I ate my crusts, and Grandpa convinced me that carrots could make me see in the dark. I'm here to tell you that you will have super-strength if you eat this spinach-loaded pasta bake.

1 broccoli, cut into large florets,
    stalk cut into chunks
1 cauliflower, cut into large florets,
    stalk cut into chunks
1 leek, chunkily chopped
1 tbsp olive oil
1 tsp garlic granules
400g (14oz) wholewheat pasta
250g (9oz) ricotta
450ml (15¼fl oz/scant 2 cups) vegetable stock
160g (5¾oz) frozen peas, thawed
15g (½oz) basil, leaves only
1 tbsp cornflour (cornstarch)
100g (3½oz) baby spinach
60g (2¼oz) almonds, finely chopped
Zest of 1 lemon
Salt and ground black pepper

Preheat the oven to 220°C (200°C fan/425°F/gas 7).

Add the broccoli, cauliflower and leek to a large roasting dish with the oil and garlic granules. Season with salt and pepper, mix to coat and roast for 25–30 minutes, stirring halfway through, until everything is starting to turn golden.

Meanwhile, bring a large pot of salted water to the boil. Add the pasta and cook for 2 minutes less than indicated on the back of the packet. Drain and set aside.

Take half your roasted veggies and blitz them in a blender with the ricotta, vegetable stock, peas, basil and cornflour. Pour back into your roasting dish with the remaining roasted veg, add the pasta and give everything a good stir.

Sprinkle on the spinach, cover the dish tightly with foil and bake for 15 minutes to wilt the spinach and make sure everything is piping hot.

Mix the almonds and lemon zest together, then sprinkle this on top of the pasta bake just before serving.

NOTES

This will keep happily in an airtight container for 3 days in the fridge. To freeze, slice the pasta bake into portions and place it in airtight containers. Freeze for up to 4 months. To reheat, remove it from the freezer the night before and place it in the fridge to thaw. Reheat in the microwave or the oven until piping hot in the centre.

One-pan Chickpea and Coconut Curry

SERVES 4 · TAKES 45 MINUTES

I'm seven years old. I've done what felt like the performance of a lifetime and taken gold at my village hall tap-dancing competition. As a reward, we pick up a curry from the local takeaway and I swap out my normal tikka for an impromptu korma. What heavenly sweet, coconutty witchcraft is this?! This one-pan wonder has those familiar nods that make me feel like I've conquered the world again... or at least smashed out a time step.

3 red onions, halved and sliced into half-moons

2 red (bell) peppers, deseeded and cut into strips

1 tbsp coconut or vegetable oil

2 garlic cloves, crushed

5cm (2in) piece of fresh ginger, peeled and grated

3 tbsp tomato paste

1 tsp chilli powder

1 tsp ground cumin

1 tsp ground turmeric

¼ tsp ground cinnamon

Seeds of 3 cardamom pods, ground (optional)

2 x 400g (14oz) cans of chickpeas

250ml (9fl oz/1 cup) coconut milk

180g (6¼oz) basmati rice

200ml (7fl oz/scant 1 cup) water

2 tsp garam masala

200g (7oz) spinach

Salt

TO SERVE

1 lemon or lime, cut into wedges

Mango chutney (optional)

Sauté the onions and peppers in a large, deep saucepan with the oil and a pinch of salt over a medium heat until softened, around 10 minutes. Stir in the garlic and ginger and cook for 1 minute, then stir through the tomato paste, cooking until the paste darkens slightly.

Add the chilli powder, cumin, turmeric, cinnamon and ground cardamom seeds, if using, and cook for a few seconds until the fragrances start to release.

Add the chickpeas and the liquid from their cans, along with the coconut milk, rice and water. Bring to the boil, then turn down to a simmer and pop a lid on the pan. Cook for 15–20 minutes, until the rice is tender.

Remove from the heat, stir in the garam masala, then add the spinach. Cover again and let sit for 10 minutes so the spinach can wilt. Give it a good stir and then serve with citrus wedges for squeezing and some mango chutney, if you like.

Catch of the Day

My summers were spent on the windy
beaches of North Wales with my
grandparents. Grandpa Rog had a little
fishing boat and he used to enter the
annual mackerel race. Afterwards, he
would exchange catches with the local
fishermen to create a seafood feast.

We'd fire up the BBQ on the beach
and open various containers of salads
and side dishes, before tucking into this
delicious spread with sandy fingers.
If we were lucky, we'd also get a plate
of vinegar-drenched chips from
the Tŷ Coch Inn.

These dishes are powered by simple
ingredients that don't require much
work to turn them into a stunning
plate of comforting delight.

Lentil and Smoked Haddock Kedgeree

SERVES 4 · TAKES 45 MINUTES

My grandpa and granny have a chest freezer that could feed their street if the apocalypse occurred. A treasure trove filled with delights from the butcher and the fishmonger, and ready-made treats for any impromptu visitor. Vibrant yellow smoked haddock will stand the test of time in your freezer, but it won't last a second when you give this recipe a go.

200g (7oz) dried green or brown lentils

2 tbsp olive oil

1 large brown onion, finely chopped

3 garlic cloves, crushed

1 tsp ground cumin

1 tsp ground coriander

1 tsp ground turmeric

½ tsp smoked paprika

450ml (15¼fl oz/scant 2 cups) vegetable stock

2 vine tomatoes, chopped

2 smoked haddock fillets, skinned and cut into 2cm (¾in) chunks

Salt and ground black pepper

FOR THE QUICK PICKLED ONION

1 red onion, halved and thinly sliced (into half-moons)

2 tbsp white wine vinegar

TO SERVE

2 hard-boiled free-range eggs (see page 79), peeled and chopped

Low-fat plain yogurt

Chopped parsley leaves

Add the sliced red onion to a bowl with the vinegar and a pinch of salt. Give the onions a good squeeze and set aside to pickle while you prepare everything else.

Rinse the lentils through and drain well. In a medium saucepan, heat the olive oil over a gentle heat. Add the onion and garlic and sauté for about 5 minutes until softened.

Add the cumin, coriander, turmeric, smoked paprika and ½ teaspoon each of salt and black pepper. Stir to combine and cook for another minute. Add the lentils along with the vegetable stock. Bring to a boil, then reduce heat to low. Cover and simmer for 15 minutes or until the lentils are tender.

Once the lentils are cooked, stir in the chopped tomatoes and smoked haddock. Cook for a further 5–7 minutes until your fish has cooked and started to delicately flake apart, adding a little more stock if the lentils start to look dry.

Serve the kedgeree topped with your quick pickled onions, the chopped hard-boiled eggs, a few dollops of yogurt and some chopped parsley.

NOTES

Quick pickled onions are one of my favourite little kitchen hacks. They are a great addition to any dish needing a little brightening. Scatter onto curries, stuff into wraps and even sprinkle on your cheese sandwich.

Fish Fingers in Mushy Pea Baps with Tartare Sauce

SERVES 4 · TAKES 2 HOURS

If there is a fish finger sandwich on the menu, Mum is having it. It's doused in nostalgia from her uni days where her finely tuned skills in the kitchen were set aside for a quick freezer dinner of fish fingers, finished with a slab of cheese melted under the grill.

20g (¾oz) plain (all-purpose) flour
1 free-range egg
100g (3½oz) cornflakes, crushed
Zest of 1 lemon
400g (14oz) sustainable white fish, sliced into fingers
Lettuce, to serve
Salt and ground black pepper

FOR THE MUSHY PEA BAPS
3g (1 tsp) fast-action dried yeast
1 tsp caster (superfine) sugar
90ml (3fl oz/6 tbsp) tepid water
1 x 300g (10½oz) can of mushy peas
1 tbsp sunflower oil, plus extra for greasing
1 tsp fine salt
150g (5½oz) wholemeal (wholewheat) flour
200g (7oz) strong white bread flour

FOR THE TARTARE SAUCE
200g (7oz) 0% fat Greek yogurt
2 heaped tbsp capers, roughly chopped
2 heaped tbsp cornichons, roughly chopped
1 shallot, finely chopped
Handful of parsley leaves, finely chopped
Juice of 1 lemon

NOTES

The baps will keep for up to 5 days in an airtight container at room temperature. They can also be frozen for up to 3 months – wrap tightly with cling film (plastic wrap) then place in a freezer bag.

If you'd prefer to air-fry your fish fingers, heat the air-fryer to 200°C/400°F and cook for 4–5 minutes, turning them halfway through.

For the baps, mix the yeast and sugar with the tepid water and allow to activate for 5–10 minutes (or until light foam appears on the surface).

Empty the can of mushy peas into a bowl and stir in the sunflower oil, giving it an extra mush as you go. Stir in your yeast mixture and the salt.

Mix the flours together and start to add them to your wet mixture, stirring until it forms a dough. Tip it out onto a work surface and knead by hand until it's soft and pliable. Pop it into a lightly oiled bowl and cover loosely with a tea (dish) towel. Set aside in a warm spot to rise (almost doubling in size) for 45–50 minutes.

Knock back the dough (this simply means another brief knead), then divide it evenly into 4 and shape each piece into a ball. Pop them on a lined baking tray, cover with the tea towel and set the tray back into its cosy spot for another 30 minutes.

Preheat the oven to 200°C (180°C fan/400°F/gas 6).

Bake the baps for 25 minutes until risen, golden and with a lovely tappable bottom.

Meanwhile, mix the ingredients for the tartare sauce together in a bowl and set aside.

We are going to pané (breadcrumb) our fish fingers. Place the flour in a shallow bowl. In another bowl whisk the egg and, in another, mix the crushed cornflakes, lemon zest and some salt and pepper. Gently pat the fish pieces dry with kitchen paper. Dip your pieces of fish in the flour, shaking off any excess, then dip in the beaten egg. Finally dip in the crushed cornflakes, ensuring the fish is completely covered.

Once they are all coated, place the fish fingers on a lightly oiled baking tray and bake for 20 minutes, turning them over halfway through so they are lovely and golden on both sides. Enjoy sandwiched within the baps with the tartare sauce and some crisp lettuce!

Prawn and Avocado Cocktail with Melba Toast

SERVES 4 · TAKES 15 MINUTES

When I think retro food, I think prawn cocktail. I think of my grandma's Martini glasses, with freshly spun iceberg lettuce, a vibrant pink pile of prawns in Marie rose sauce with a sprinkle of paprika and a wedge of lemon, and some buttered bread on the side.

1 avocado, peeled, halved and pitted

120g (4¼oz) 0% fat Greek yogurt

3 tbsp tomato ketchup

1 tbsp horseradish sauce

1 tsp Worcestershire sauce

Tabasco sauce, to taste

Pinch of white pepper

300g (10½oz) cooked peeled prawns (shrimp)

8 thin slices of wholemeal bread

½ iceberg lettuce

Paprika or cayenne, for dusting

Lemon wedges, to serve

Add half an avocado, the yogurt, ketchup, horseradish, Worcestershire sauce, Tabasco and white pepper to a blender and blitz until smooth. Have a taste and season as required. Add to a bowl with the prawns and stir to coat.

It's best to do the Melba toast under a hot grill (broiler). Toast the bread slices until golden brown on both sides, then slice each in half into triangles. Next, carefully cut the toast slices through the middle horizontally using a bread knife – as if opening a pita bread – so each slice becomes two much thinner slices. Each slice should now have a toasted side and a soft side. Scrape off any soft bread from the soft sides of the slices and discard (in your mouth). Grill the soft sides until golden brown too.

Shred the iceberg lettuce and thinly slice your remaining avocado half, then divide between 4 serving glasses. Add a small pile of saucy prawns to each, then dust with paprika or cayenne. Serve with the Melba toast alongside and lemon wedges for squeezing.

NOTES

Serve the lettuce on ice for added eccentricity!

CATCH OF THE DAY

CATCH OF THE DAY

Tuna Pesto Picnic Pasta Salad

SERVES 4 · TAKES 15 MINUTES

Whenever Mum took my brother and me out for the day as kids, there would always be a tuna pasta salad packed into a Tupperware surrounded by ice packs in the bottom of a supermarket carrier bag. It needed to last at least 4 hours, as this was how long it would take for my mum to wrangle me and my brother away from the playground to recharge ourselves with lunch and a drink of water to calm our flushed faces.

250g (9oz) dried pasta (penne, conchiglie, fusilli)

120g (4¼oz) frozen petits pois

100g (3½oz) spinach

½ bunch of basil, leaves only

30g (1oz) Parmesan, finely grated

Juice of ½ lemon

4 heaped tbsp 0% fat Greek yogurt

¼ tsp ground black pepper

1 small red onion, finely diced

1 tbsp capers

2 tbsp cornichons, roughly chopped

80g (2¾oz) pitted black olives, roughly chopped

2 x 145g (5oz) cans of tuna in spring water, drained

Cook the pasta in boiling salted water until just past al dente (as pasta cools it firms up a little again, so you don't want too much bite), adding the petits pois for the last couple of minutes. Drain and rinse thoroughly with cold water.

Add the spinach, basil, Parmesan, lemon juice, yogurt and black pepper to a blender and blitz into a smooth, vibrant, green dressing.

Add the dressing to a large bowl with your pasta and peas, and all the remaining ingredients. Stir well and tuck in (or pack into Tupperware ready for your picnic).

NOTES

Tuna in spring water doesn't have any added fats (like when in sunflower oil) or salt (like when in brine).

Grilled Mango and Prawn Noodle Salad

SERVES 4 · TAKES 20 MINUTES

It's easy to be lazy at lunchtime. If the day has run away with me, then I often default to a bowl of cereal... but when I remember this recipe exists, there really are no excuses.

150g (5½oz) sugar snap peas
4 bundles of wholewheat noodles
½ mango, cubed
2 carrots, julienned
1 cucumber, halved lengthways, deseeded (using a teaspoon) and julienned (see Note on page 84)
Handful of coriander (cilantro), roughly chopped
Handful of roasted cashew nuts, roughly chopped
300g (10½oz) cooked peeled prawns (shrimp)
Salt

FOR THE DRESSING
2 heaped tbsp tahini
Juice of 1 lime
1 red chilli (or as much as you can handle)
2 tbsp light soy sauce
1 tbsp sesame oil
½ ripe mango

Make the dressing first by blitzing all the ingredients in a blender. Set aside.

Add the sugar snap peas and noodles to a pan of boiling, salted water and cook until the noodles have softened, then drain.

Meanwhile, heat a griddle pan (or frying pan) until hot, add the diced mango and grill for 1–2 minutes on each side to get light scorch marks. The natural sugars in the mango will caramelize and add a lovely depth of flavour to the salad.

In a large bowl toss the sugar snaps and noodles with the dressing, then chuck in the carrots, cucumber, coriander, cashews, prawns and mango. Add salt to taste, then mix well.

NOTES

If you don't want to bother grilling your mango, simply add it raw – it'll still be delicious.

CATCH OF THE DAY

CATCH OF THE DAY

Squeaky Thai-style Fish Cakes

SERVES 4 · TAKES 30 MINUTES

Back in the early days of my house share, there was a battle for space in the matchbox-sized freezer. By default, there would be several indecently large Tupperware containers of batch-cooked chilli, exploded beer yet to be cleaned up and some stray chips from a thrown-together dinner thanks to the local convenience store. But I saved my spot for fish cakes.

You will need a food processor for this recipe – it breaks down the proteins in the fish to help your fish cakes bind and give that delightfully springy texture – but I promise it's worth it. Easy, hearty and superbly freezer-friendly.

400g (14oz) responsibly sourced fish, deboned and skinless (bass, cod, hake)
2 tbsp Thai red curry paste
1 tbsp light soy sauce
Juice of ½ lime
80g (2¾oz) fine green beans, finely chopped
1 tbsp olive oil
Coriander (cilantro) leaves, to serve
Lime wedges, for squeezing

FOR THE DIPPING SAUCE
2 tbsp fish sauce
Juice of 2 limes
2 green chillies, finely chopped
3 spring onions (scallions), finely sliced
1 garlic clove, crushed
2 tsp brown sugar
2 tbsp water

Chuck everything for the dipping sauce into a bowl and stir. Set aside to allow the flavours to infuse.

Place the fish, curry paste, soy and lime juice into a food processor and blitz. I like to check my seasoning at this point by frying a small amount of the mixture in a pan and giving it a taste, then adding more soy or lime if needed.

Mix the fine green beans into the fish mixture by hand, giving everything a squeeze until evenly distributed. With damp hands (much easier), form the mixture into 8 patties flattened to a 2.5cm (1in) thickness.

Heat the oil in a large frying pan over a medium heat and add the fish cakes. Cook for 5 minutes until golden, flip and then cook for a further 3–5 minutes on the other side until cooked through.

Serve the fish cakes scattered with coriander and with lime wedges for squeezing, then tear and dip into the dipping sauce while still hot.

NOTES

These can be frozen, uncooked, for up to 3 months. To reheat from frozen, remove them from the freezer and let them thaw in the fridge overnight. Alternatively, if you're in a hurry, you can defrost them in the microwave on a low setting. Once defrosted, cook as above.

Lime-infused Salmon Skewers with Jalapeño Dip

SERVES 4 · TAKES 25 MINUTES

Not everyone is a fan of fish, and if your introduction to a flaky fillet is that of week-old supermarket salmon that smells strongly of a used wellington boot, then I understand. But have you ever tried freshly caught fish? It's unparalleled. The freshest I ever tasted was in my mother-in-law's home town in Sardinia. I remember revelling in a wonderful lunch at her favourite trattoria, my Italian surprisingly improving with every glass of wine. The sparkling highlight of the feast was a fish so fresh they must have lassoed it straight from sea to plate. Served with a cold glass of wine, I challenge you not to become a fish convert in this scenario. And while these salmon skewers aren't Italian, they were born out of my need to inject the bright, vibrant freshness of a morning catch into your supermarket-purchased fish.

Zest and juice of 4 limes
100ml (3½fl oz/scant ½ cup) fish stock
1 celery stick, grated
1 garlic clove, crushed
2.5cm (1in) piece of fresh ginger,
　peeled and grated
Pinch of salt
4 responsibly sourced salmon fillets,
　cubed into hearty chunks
1 large red onion, peeled, quartered
　and pulled into petals

FOR THE JALAPEÑO DIP
2 tbsp fish sauce
3 tbsp sliced green jalapeños in brine
2 tbsp jalapeño brine from the jar
Juice of 2 limes
1 tsp sugar

Add the lime zest and juice, fish stock, celery, garlic, ginger and salt to a large bowl and mix. Add the salmon cubes and onion petals and let them rest in the marinade for 10–15 minutes, giving them an occasional toss.

Take some soaked wooden skewers and slide on the salmon and onion petals, alternating between each. In a hot pan or on the BBQ (grill), cook the skewers for 2–3 minutes until golden on all sides. Discard your leftover marinade.

For the dip, mix together the fish sauce, jalapeños, jalapeño brine, lime juice and sugar in a small bowl. Check for seasoning, adding more sugar or lime juice as needed, then serve alongside the hot salmon skewers.

NOTES

Check your wooden skewers fit your pan/grill and cut down to size before adding the fish to them if necessary.

Firm, robust fish stands up best to barbecuing (grilling). Halibut, monkfish and swordfish are all good candidates. More delicate types of fish, such as cod, can easily flake and fall through the grill, although with a little prep and care when cooking, most fish can be barbecued.

If cooking fish on the BBQ, oil the grill directly and get your grill very hot first to avoid sticking.

CATCH OF THE DAY

Mackerel Fish Tacos
with Corn Salsa

SERVES 4 · TAKES 30 MINUTES

My fondest memories of Grandpa Bryher were at the fishing lakes. We'd pitch up with our fold-out chairs, a box of muddled reels and colourful fishing flies. Tobacco smoke billowed from his pipe as the whizz of the line cast out into the lake. We'd sit quietly for hours with the occasional nod to the fishermen docking nearby. I can't eat fish without seeing his wink and hearing the click of his tongue on his teeth as he would proudly reel in the first catch of the day.

2 large wholemeal tortilla wraps
Olive oil, for brushing
1 tsp ground cumin
1 tsp chilli powder
1 tsp ground coriander
8 mackerel fillets
Salt and ground black pepper

FOR THE CORN SALSA
1 x 325g (11½oz) can of sweetcorn,
    drained and rinsed
1 red onion, finely chopped
Zest and juice of 2 limes
1 red chilli, finely chopped
2 large tomatoes, deseeded and finely chopped
½ bunch of coriander (cilantro), finely chopped

TO SERVE
½ iceberg lettuce, finely shredded
80g (2¾oz) sour cream
Spring onions (scallions) and chillies,
    to garnish (optional)

Preheat the oven to 200°C (180°C fan/400°F/gas 6).

To make your taco shells, brush the tortilla wraps lightly with oil. Use a muffin or cupcake tray and flip it over so the moulds of the tray are poking up. Cut each wrap into quarters and push each one between four of the moulds so it bends into a cup shape. Bake in the oven for 8–10 minutes, then remove and allow to cool before removing them; you should have crispy shells.

Add all your ingredients for the salsa to a bowl and give a good toss to combine. Have a taste and add a touch of salt or pepper if needed.

Preheat a pan (ideally a griddle pan) over a high heat.

Mix the spices together in a bowl, then sprinkle this all over your mackerel fillets. Season the fillets with salt and pepper, then place them in the hot pan. Cook on one side for 2–3 minutes before flipping and cooking for a final minute. Don't overcrowd your pan – if you need to, cook the fish in batches.

To serve, pop some lettuce into the base of each taco cup, then break up the mackerel and add this on top. Sprinkle generously with the corn salsa and top with a teaspoon of sour cream. Spring onions and sliced chilli will add a lovely, colourful garnish, if you're feeling fancy!

Mauritian Fish Curry with a Zingy Coriander Drizzle

SERVES 4 · TAKES 40 MINUTES

My brother and sister-in-law married in an intimate ceremony in Mauritius. It was paradise in every way – the crystal-clear waters bouncing bright sunlight around luscious green landscapes. And the food! Their wedding meal was a Mauritian fish curry, and when we celebrate their anniversary, I am, in many ways, also celebrating the discovery of this comforting dish.

2 aubergines (eggplants), cut into large chunks

2 tbsp olive oil

1 tsp ground cumin

1 tsp ground coriander

4 responsibly sourced white fish fillets (halibut, bass, snapper, cod)

2 tbsp cornflour (cornstarch), seasoned with salt and black pepper

Juice of 1 lemon

1 red onion, halved and thinly sliced into half-moons

4 fresh curry leaves (or 6 dried if you can't find fresh)

5cm (2in) piece of fresh ginger, grated

3 garlic cloves, crushed

1 red chilli, finely sliced (or more if you fancy more spice)

2 tbsp medium curry powder

4 large tomatoes, roughly chopped

100ml (3½fl oz/scant ½ cup) water

Salt

Poppadoms, crushed

0% fat Greek yogurt, to serve

FOR THE CORIANDER DRIZZLE

Large bunch of coriander (cilantro)

8–10 mint leaves

Juice of 1 lime

3 tbsp olive oil

3 tbsp water

Preheat the oven to 230°C (210°C fan/450°F/gas 8).

Place the aubergines in a roasting dish and toss with 1 tablespoon of the oil, the cumin and coriander. Roast for 20–25 minutes, tossing halfway through.

Pat dry the fish fillets with kitchen paper, then dust them with the seasoned cornflour. Heat a large pan over a medium heat with the remaining tablespoon of olive oil. Add your fish and cook for 2 minutes. Squeeze over the lemon juice, then flip the fish and cook for another 2 minutes. Your fish should start to flake when you prick it with a fork. Depending on the thickness of your fillets, this may take a little longer. Remove from the pan and set aside.

To the same pan, add the sliced onion and curry leaves with a pinch of salt and a splash of water. Allow the onion to soften for 10 minutes and catch a light golden hue, then add the ginger, garlic, chilli and curry powder. Stir and cook for 2–3 minutes. Stir in the tomatoes, then cover and cook for 3–4 minutes. Add the water, the fish and the aubergine, cover again and simmer for 10–15 minutes so the sauce thickens and the flavours infuse. You can add more water for a saucier curry or serve it up a little thicker (that's how I like it).

Meanwhile, add the coriander drizzle ingredients to a blender and blitz until smooth.

Serve the curry with the coriander drizzle over the top and finish with some crushed poppadoms and dollops of yogurt.

NOTES

The curry will keep in an airtight container in the fridge for 2–3 days. When reheating, I recommend doing so on the stove in a pan set over a low heat, stirring occasionally until it reaches a safe internal temperature (74°C/165°F).

CATCH OF THE DAY

CATCH OF THE DAY

Spiced Hake en Papillote with a Cauliflower Crumb

SERVES 4 · TAKES 1 HOUR

Dad is well versed in the classics, having worked in a traditional bistro (the kind with dated Victorian décor and frills on the turkey legs at Christmas), and I've learned many staple techniques from him over the years. Though it sounds snooty to be serving up 'en papillote', some of the finest French techniques make the most simple and obvious sense. Steaming your fish in its own little bag locks in flavour and nutrients and ensures perfectly flaky fish every time.

½ tsp ground turmeric

1 tsp paprika

1 tsp ground cinnamon

2 tsp garam masala

80g (2¾oz) sultanas (golden raisins)

1 x 400g (14oz) can of chickpeas, drained and rinsed

1 courgette (zucchini), thinly sliced

1 tbsp olive oil

4 responsibly sourced hake fillets

4 coin-sized discs of fresh ginger

1 lemon, thinly sliced

Salt and ground black pepper

FOR THE CAULIFLOWER CRUMB

½ cauliflower

60g (2¼oz) hazelnuts

NOTES

The term 'en papillote' literally translates to 'in parchment'. This method of cooking is often used for fish, chicken and vegetables. One of the key benefits of cooking en papillote is that it allows for healthy and flavoursome cooking without added fats or oils. The steam created by the enclosed pouch helps to keep the food moist and tender, while also infusing it with flavour from any seasonings added to the pouch.

Preheat the oven to 240°C (220°C fan/475°F/gas 9).

Whizz the cauliflower and hazelnuts in a blender, then scatter in a thin layer onto a large baking tray lined with baking paper. Bake for 30–35 minutes, tossing halfway through, until golden and crisp. Remove and set aside, then lower the oven temperature to 220°C (200°C fan/425°F/gas 7).

Add the ground spices, sultanas, chickpeas and courgette to a bowl with the oil. Give everything a good mix to evenly coat.

Take 4 large sheets of baking paper and divide the spiced vegetables equally between each sheet, creating small piles in the middle of the baking paper. Sit a fish fillet on top with 1 disc of ginger and 2–3 slices of lemon overlapping on top of the fish. Sprinkle with salt and pepper.

Working one parcel at a time, bring the widest edges of your baking paper up over your fish so they meet. Using small folds, start to roll the two edges down to seal the top of your parcel. Next, either twist or fold the open ends of your parcel to fully seal it. Although you want your parcel securely closed, you need to allow a little bit of room within it for the air to expand and circulate, so no need to tuck your fish in too tight.

Pop the sealed parcels on a baking tray and place in the oven for 12–15 minutes. Being careful of the hot steam, open your parcels. Everything should be juicy and fragrant. Sprinkle over the cauliflower crumb to serve.

Fish Pie with Colcannon Mash

SERVES 4 · TAKES 1 HOUR 30 MINUTES

'Show us your mussels, now show us your cockles,' – a one-liner from my foul-mouthed Irish great-grandmother and a treasured catchphrase when it comes to slinging together our favourite seafood for a stunning supper.

500ml (17fl oz/2 cups) skimmed milk (or dairy-free alternative)
750g (1lb 10½oz) responsibly sourced fish fillets (I like an even split of cod, salmon and smoked haddock)
2 garlic cloves, peeled
1 brown onion, peeled and quartered
1 bay leaf
4 large hard-boiled free-range eggs (see page 79), plunged into cold water to stop them cooking
1 tsp olive oil
3 tbsp plain (all-purpose) flour
200g (7oz) frozen peas
Juice of 1 lemon
Salt and ground black pepper

FOR THE COLCANNON MASH
2 leeks, finely chopped
½ white cabbage, finely chopped
30g (1oz) butter
1 tsp olive oil
500g (1lb 2oz) potatoes, unpeeled, cut into 4cm (1½in) cubes
140g (5oz) 0% fat Greek yogurt
Handful of dill, finely chopped
Handful of chives, finely chopped

Preheat the oven to 220°C (200°C fan/425°F/gas 7).

Add the chopped leeks and cabbage to a roasting dish with the butter, oil and a generous pinch of salt. Give everything a good mix and then seal your roasting dish with foil and place in the oven for 45 minutes.

Meanwhile, add the potatoes to a pan of boiling salted water and cook until tender, about 15–20 minutes. Drain and allow to air-dry in the pan.

When the cabbage and leeks are cooked, add them to the potatoes and give everything a good crush with a masher. Beat in the yogurt, dill and chives using a wooden spoon. Taste and season with salt and pepper.

To make your pie filling, add the milk to a pan with the fish, garlic, onion and bay leaf. Bring to a boil, then drop to a simmer for 6–7 minutes.

Strain the infused milk into another saucepan, catching the fish in a sieve (strainer) – make sure you don't lose any of that liquid! Remove the onion and garlic and set them to one side. Discard the bay leaf.

When the fish is cool enough to handle, discard the skin, then break up the flesh into roughly 4cm (1½in) pieces and add it to a pie dish. Peel and halve your eggs and add them to the pie dish, too.

When the onion is cool enough, finely chop it and crush the garlic. Add these to a frying pan with the oil and flour and stir well. Gradually add the infused milk mixture to the pan a little at a time, stirring as it thickens, until you've used up all the milk. Add the frozen peas and cook for 2–3 minutes more, stirring occasionally.

Recipe continues overleaf.

CATCH OF THE DAY

Pour the sauce over your fish and eggs in the pie dish, then squeeze over the lemon juice.

Spoon the colcannon mash over the pie filling, then transfer the pie to the oven – still at 220°C (200°C fan/425°F/gas 7) – for 20–25 minutes, until it is golden brown and bubbling.

NOTES

If you have leftovers (which you likely will as this is a generous dish!), it's important the cooked fish pie is cooled as quickly as possible then covered and refrigerated, or put in the freezer. If you're not planning to eat it in the next few days, then freezing is best. Portion up your leftover pie into airtight containers and freeze for up to 1 month.

The fish will be drier when reheated, but it should still taste delicious. To reheat, add it to an oven dish and cover with foil. Bake until piping hot all the way through.

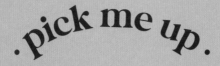

Lemony Smoked Salmon Mousse

SERVES 4 · TAKES 10 MINUTES

I used to play restaurants with my friends growing up. We would create menus, provide entertainment (a dance to the latest Steps track), prepare a 3-course feast and serve it while donning our dads' waistcoats and ties, and even deliver a bill at the end of the meal, despite our parents paying for the food shop. One of the signature starters of 'The Callson' or 'La Martson' restaurants was our salmon mousse. And yes, it's simple enough that a child could prepare it!

200g (7oz) smoked salmon
200g (7oz) 0% fat Greek yogurt
1 tbsp lemon juice
Salt and ground black pepper
Small handful of dill, chopped, to garnish

Remove any skin or bones from the smoked salmon and roughly chop it into pieces.

Add to a food processor or blender with the yogurt and lemon juice and blend until smooth and creamy, then season to taste. I like to decant into individual ramekins, so I have single portions for a quick snack, or to serve at a dinner party. Before serving, garnish with fresh dill for an added touch of freshness and flavour.

Serve chilled with your choice of crackers, bread or crudités.

CATCH OF THE DAY

Squid and Samphire Risotto with Lemon Gremolata

SERVES 4 · TAKES 45 MINUTES

I'm an impatient cook. Lingering around the pot smelling all the good smells yet unable to eat it is a true test of stamina, but for some dishes I accept that patience is required. So go ahead, risotto, take your time – I know it's only going to make you more delicious.

1 large brown onion, finely diced
2 celery sticks, finely diced
Splash of olive oil
2 garlic cloves, finely diced
350g (12oz) arborio rice (risotto rice)
3 tbsp white wine vinegar
1l (35fl oz/4 cups) hot fish stock
300g (10½oz) frozen squid rings
150g (5½oz) peas
90g (4¼oz) samphire
Salt and ground white pepper
Squeeze of lemon juice, to finish

FOR THE LEMON GREMOLATA
Zest of 1 lemon
2 garlic cloves, peeled
Bunch of flat-leaf parsley, leaves only

For the gremolata, either chop everything finely and smash it together with the flat side of your knife on a chopping board, or bung it all in a food processor and blitz. Place in a bowl and set aside.

In a large, deep frying pan set over a medium heat, add the onion and celery with the splash of oil and soften for 10–12 minutes until translucent. Stir in the garlic and rice, cook for 1 minute, then turn the heat up and add the vinegar to deglaze the pan.

Reduce the heat to low–medium and start to add the hot fish stock, a ladleful at a time, stirring continuously to encourage the starch out of the rice.

Once all your stock has been used up, have a taste and check the rice is soft but with a little bit of bite. If you need to cook it longer, simply add splashes of boiling water to keep it moist. The texture you want is for the rice to fall slowly off the back of a spoon, leaving a glossy, saucy trail. Not claggy, not soupy.

Scatter the frozen squid over the top of the risotto, cover with a lid and cook for 3 minutes. This will steam your frozen squid. Add the peas, give everything a good stir, cover and cook for another 3 minutes. Finally, stir in the samphire, cover and cook for 2 minutes. Adding your ingredients in stages will ensure the temperature of your pan doesn't drop too dramatically, cooking your squid but keeping it tender and ensuring vibrant greens that still have crunch.

Add a squeeze of lemon, season with white pepper and salt, then sprinkle over the gremolata.

NOTE

Risotto has a creamy texture and taste, not from the addition of cream but from the slow release of starches from the rice grains as they cook in the stock. That's why the more slowly you cook it, the creamier it will be.

Steamed Mussels with Spinach and Parsley Pikelets

SERVES 4 · TAKES 45 MINUTES

I am transported to the seaside every time I eat mussels. They remind me of fishing in the rockpools in Wales, finding tiny shells housing unexpected creatures and creating colourful collages on the sand with washed-up seaweed. In our trunks and towels, we would skip to a beach café and order the freshest mussels in a generous garlicky broth, mopped up with a large hunk of doughy baguette.

1 tsp olive oil
1 brown onion, finely chopped
1 celery stick, finely chopped
3 garlic cloves, chopped
3 tbsp white wine vinegar
150ml (5fl oz/scant ⅔ cup) hot fish stock
2kg (2lb 5oz) fresh mussels in shells, cleaned
    (see Note)

FOR THE SPINACH AND PARSLEY PIKELETS
100g (3½oz) self-raising flour
1 tsp baking powder
Pinch of salt
120g (4¼oz) baby spinach
Bunch of parsley (leaves and stalks), chopped
50ml (1¾fl oz/3½ tbsp) skimmed milk
    (or dairy-free alternative)
1 large free-range egg
Low-calorie oil spray, for frying

TO FINISH
Parsley leaves, chopped
Squeeze of lemon juice
30g (1oz) butter

To make the pikelets, add the flour, baking powder and salt to a bowl. Blitz the spinach, parsley, milk and egg together in a blender until smooth. Whisk your wet and dry mixtures together into a smooth batter.

Spritz a non-stick frying pan with some low-calorie spray. In batches, add spoonfuls of the pikelet batter and cook for 1–2 minutes until bubbles form on the surface. Flip and cook for another minute on the other side. Once cooked, pop your pikelets into a clean tea (dish) towel to keep warm.

For the mussels, heat the oil in a large pan that has a well-fitting lid. Add the onion and celery and cook over a gentle heat for 10 minutes until soft. Add the garlic and vinegar and turn up the heat to lightly deglaze the pan. Add the hot fish stock.

When the stock starts to boil, add the mussels to the pan and turn the heat to low. Put the lid on and let the mussels steam for 4–5 minutes. You will know they're cooked when all the shells have opened. Any that remain closed should be discarded.

Scatter with the chopped parsley, add a squeeze of lemon and the butter and give everything a final toss. Serve with the delicious little pikelets to help mop up the juices.

NOTE

To prep your mussels, wash them under plenty of cold, running water. Discard any open ones that won't close when lightly squeezed. Pull out the tough, fibrous beards protruding from between the tightly closed shells and then knock off any barnacles with a large knife. Give the mussels another quick rinse to remove any little pieces of shell.

Friday Night In

It's Friday night. The working week is in the
rear-view mirror, and two golden days of
freedom lie ahead of you. You need something
celebratory, dishes to tuck into that feel like
a figurative gear change as you accelerate into
the weekend. It's Friday Night Takeaway time.

When I was little, I loved the ritual of poring
over the takeaway menus that had been posted
through the door, figuring out whether we
were feeling pizza, Chinese or Indian that
night, before arguing over whether it would
be my brother or me who would accompany
Dad in the car to go and collect it.

This chapter is all about capturing the magic
of those Friday nights, minus the increasingly
hefty price tag, the impossibly long wait times,
the complaints about dishes turning up cold
and the next day's inevitable stuffed-crust
hangover – with no sacrifices in flavour
or happiness.

Homemade Tortilla Chip Nachos with Chilli

SERVES 4 · TAKES 25 MINUTES

The first time you're allowed to take the bus into town as a teenager is a massive moment. We'd gone 'shopping' and if we wanted to afford those combat trousers and butterfly hair clips, we were going to have to share lunch. Nachos became a staple – but I'm sure my homemade version is a lot better for me than what I was consuming as a teenager!

8 wholemeal tortilla wraps
½ quantity of charred chilli pepper con carne (page 56)
1 quantity of creamy avocado dip (page 85)
40g (1½oz) Cheddar, grated
1 spring onion (scallion), chopped
1 large tomato, deseeded and diced

Preheat the oven to 240°C (220°C fan/475°F/gas 9).

Cut each tortilla wrap into 8 triangles and arrange in a single layer on a large baking tray (or split between two trays). Bake in the oven for 10 minutes until golden and crisp, then set aside to cool and harden.

Add a layer of the hardened tortilla chips to an ovenproof serving dish. Spoon over some chilli con carne, then dollop over some avocado dip. Add another layer of tortilla chips, then repeat the topping (try to do 2–3 layers). Finish by scattering over the cheese.

Bake in the oven for 10 minutes until the cheese has melted, then finish with a sprinkle of spring onions and diced tomato.

Poppadom Nachos with Shredded Curry Chicken

SERVES 4 · TAKES 1 HOUR 10 MINUTES

I love the satisfying strike to the centre of the poppadom stack whenever we go to an Indian restaurant. If you're lucky you break it perfectly all the way through into large shards, ideal for scooping up the chutneys and raita. Sometimes it's a shattered mess, but I will always be there to pick up the pieces.

4 boneless, skinless chicken breasts

1 brown onion, chopped

2 tbsp mild curry powder

1 tsp ground cumin

1 tsp ground coriander

200ml (7fl oz/scant 1 cup) passata
    (puréed, strained tomatoes)

100ml (3½fl oz/scant ½ cup) water

100ml (3½fl oz/scant ½ cup) low-fat natural yogurt

Zest and juice of 1 lime

8 poppadoms

2 spring onions (scallions), finely chopped

½ bunch coriander (cilantro), leaves only,
    finely chopped

Salt and ground black pepper

Preheat the oven to 220°C (200°C fan/425°F/gas 7).

Rub the chicken and onion with the curry powder, cumin and coriander and season generously with salt and pepper. Place snugly into a small ovenproof dish with the passata and water and cover the dish tightly with foil.

Bake for 45 minutes, then remove the foil and bake for a further 15 minutes. Shred the cooked chicken using 2 forks and stir back through the sauce in the dish.

In a bowl, stir together the yogurt, lime zest and juice, and ¼ teaspoon of black pepper.

Gently warm the poppadoms in the oven, then break into large shards and add a layer to a serving dish. Splodge on some of your shredded chicken and a few dollops of zingy yogurt. Repeat with more poppadoms, chicken and yogurt, until it's all used up. Sprinkle over the spring onions and coriander, then serve.

Pizza Party

MAKES ENOUGH FOR 4 PIZZAS · TAKES 6+ HOURS

Wholemeal Pizza Dough

There are some foods I am not willing to compromise on and a proper yeasted pizza dough is one of them. It's just not pizza otherwise. I find there is a relaxing ritual to making pizza dough, so if you're a 'last-minute Mary' then steal yourself a day of pottering and make a batch for the freezer!

3g (1 tsp) fast-action dried yeast
420ml (14¼fl oz/generous 1¾ cups) tepid water
500g (1lb 2oz) wholemeal (wholewheat) flour,
    plus extra for dusting
2 tsp fine sea salt
Oil, for greasing

Mix the yeast and tepid water and set it aside for 5 minutes. Bubbles should form on the surface.

Mix the flour and salt in a large bowl or the bowl of a stand mixer, being sure to disperse the salt, as this can stop the yeast from working.

Tip the yeasted water into the flour and bring it together using a dinner knife. If using a stand mixer, use the paddle attachment. Once it comes together into a rough dough, allow it to rest for 30 minutes (wholemeal flour takes a little longer to absorb moisture, so it needs a bit of a rest before we start kneading and playing with the structure).

If using a stand mixer, switch to the dough hook, then knead at a medium speed for 7–10 minutes. If kneading by hand, tip the dough out onto a flat, lightly oiled work surface. It will be sticky but try to avoid dusting with flour at this stage – bench scrapers will be your best friend. Knead for 10–15 minutes. The more you work it the easier it will become to handle (but it will always be a sticky dough). You know it's done when it's shiny and smooth.

SAME-DAY DOUGH – FAST FERMENT FOR DELICIOUS PIZZA AND NO WAITING

Shape the dough into one big ball and pop it into a lightly oiled airtight container or bowl covered in cling film (plastic wrap). Leave at room temperature for 3–4 hours until more than doubled in size.

Remove and tip out onto a lightly floured work surface and separate into 4 equal pieces. Shape each into a ball – the rounder the better – tucking the dough under itself to give a tight ball. Try not to incorporate the flour into the dough, keep it on the work surface. Leave at room temperature, covered by a damp tea (dish) towel, for 1 hour 30 minutes. It is now ready to stretch, top and cook (see page 142).

NEXT-DAY DOUGH – SLOW FERMENT FOR A SOFTER, MORE FLAVOURSOME PIZZA

Shape the dough into one big ball and pop it into a lightly oiled airtight container or bowl covered in cling film (plastic wrap). Leave at room temperature for 1 hour; it should double in size.

Pop in the fridge overnight. If you have the time, 24 hours is ideal (but don't push it past 48 hours).

Remove from the fridge and leave for 2 hours to return to room temperature.

Tip the dough out onto a lightly floured work surface and separate into 4 pieces, shaping into balls as directed above. Leave at room temperature, covered by a damp tea towel for 1 hour 30 minutes. It is now ready to stretch, top and cook (see page 142).

MAKE FOR THE FREEZER – YOU CAN
STASH THESE AND USE THEM WHENEVER
THE PIZZA MOOD TAKES YOU

Shape the dough into one big ball and pop it
into a lightly oiled airtight container or bowl
covered in cling film (plastic wrap). Leave at
room temperature for 3–4 hours until more than
doubled in size. Divide it into 4 equal pieces,
shape into balls and place each ball in a separate,
lightly oiled container with a lid. You can freeze
your dough for up to 3 months.

When you want to make pizza, simply remove a
dough ball from the freezer and thaw in the fridge
overnight for best results. Once defrosted, take the
dough out of the fridge and let it come to room
temperature (this will take about 4–5 hours).
When your dough has doubled in size, it is ready
to stretch, top and cook.

Essential Pizza Sauce

**Pizza parties are how we feed most of our
friends and family. There's something about the
ritual of rolling out the dough and then debating
what the next topping should be. It's food made
to be shared!**

1 x 400g (14oz) can of high-quality plum tomatoes
1 tbsp extra virgin olive oil
1 tsp dried oregano
½ tsp salt

Chop off and discard the stalky ends off your
tomatoes (yep, even the canned ones still have
them), then finely chop. Mix in the rest of the
ingredients and your sauce is ready!

NOTES

Store the pizza sauce in an airtight container
in the fridge for 5–7 days. I freeze it in ice-cube
or muffin trays, then bag it up, so I have easy access
to individual portions. Thaw overnight in the fridge
or simply melt it in a saucepan over a low heat.

BONUS HIDDEN PASTA SAUCE

**I often freeze any leftover pizza sauce and end
up with a stash that needs using up. This is the
perfect way to do it!**

1 tsp olive oil
1 brown onion, finely diced
1 carrot, finely diced
1 courgette (zucchini), finely diced
3 garlic cloves, crushed
400ml (14fl oz/1¾ cups) pizza sauce (see left)
100ml (3½fl oz/scant ½ cup) water
30g (1oz) Parmesan, grated
Basil leaves, chopped, to serve

Add the oil to a pan with the onion and carrot.
Cook for 10 minutes until soft, then add the
courgette and garlic and cook for 3–4 minutes
until starting to turn golden.

Pour in the pizza sauce and water. Allow it to
gently simmer for 10–15 minutes, then use to coat
your choice of cooked pasta. Finish with a light
sprinkle of Parmesan and some chopped basil.

Cooking and Topping Your Pizza

Don't get mad, but as much as I stick to my guns about the importance of a quality pizza base, I am a pineapple-on-pizza kind of gal. I think you should enjoy the freedom of flavouring your pizza exactly how you like it.

Preheat the oven to 260°C (240°C fan/500°F/gas 10) – or as hot as your oven will go if it doesn't reach this temperature. Make sure you have one or two flat baking trays preheating in there, too. If any of your baking trays have sides to them, flip them upside down to create a flat surface.

Roll the dough out to 5mm (¼in) thick. I do this by hand, by stretching the dough into a circle and keeping the edge a little thicker for the crust.

Transfer the dough to a sheet of baking paper dusted with flour, on a chopping board (there's method in my specificity). Top with your sauce and toppings of choice. Swiftly and carefully open the oven and slide your pizza on its paper onto one of the hot baking trays. Close the door and cook for 8–10 minutes. Keep an eye and do give it a spin halfway through if needed.

COURGETTE, MASCARPONE AND FRIED EGG TOPPING

½ courgette (zucchini)
Handful of mint leaves, finely chopped
Juice of 1 lemon
1 tsp olive oil
Pinch of salt
1 large spoonful of pizza sauce (see page 141)
4 tsp mascarpone
1 large free-range egg
20g (¾oz) pecorino

Using a swivel vegetable peeler, peel lengthways ribbons of courgette into a bowl. Add the mint, lemon juice, oil and salt and give everything a toss through. Set aside.

Top your base with a spoonful of pizza sauce, leaving only a thin exposed border, then dot on the mascarpone. Bake for 5 minutes before carefully cracking an egg into the centre of the pizza and returning it to the oven for 3–5 minutes.

To serve, surround the egg with the zesty courgette and grate over some pecorino.

TUNA AND ONION TOPPING

½ red onion, thinly sliced into half-moons
3 tbsp white wine vinegar
Pinch of sugar
1 large spoonful of pizza sauce (see page 141)
½ x 145g (5oz) can of tuna in spring water, drained
60g (2¼oz) mozzarella (ideally pizza mozzarella as it has less moisture), cubed
Handful of black olives
Cracked black pepper

Mix the onion in a bowl with the vinegar and sugar. Give it a good squeeze and let it sit for at least 15 minutes.

Meanwhile, top your base with a spoonful of pizza sauce, leaving only a thin exposed border, then scatter over the tuna, mozzarella and olives. Bake for 8–10 minutes. Sprinkle over your pickled onions and some cracked black pepper to serve.

FIG AND RICOTTA TOPPING

1 fig, sliced into 8
1 tsp olive oil
1 thyme sprig, leaves only
1 large spoonful of pizza sauce (see page 141)
60g (2¼oz) ricotta
2 strips of Parma ham

Mix the sliced figs in a bowl with the oil and thyme. Top your base with a spoonful of pizza sauce, leaving only a thin exposed border, then dot over the ricotta. Add the figs and bake for 8–10 minutes. Drape with Parma ham and serve.

Cheat's Tortilla Pizzas 3 Ways

MAKES 4 · TAKES 10 MINUTES

When I started university, I asked my parents to write down as many recipes as they could. There were bold plans to send me on my way with a full booklet of favourites, but it became more of an 'on demand' service. Except, that is, for one typo-riddled recipe scrawled into a fresh jotter prepped for my arrival – 'flemquiche' (*flammkuchen*). My dad's version was very simply and inauthentically topped tortillas, and you needn't fix what isn't broken.

I love authentic pizza (as is demonstrated on the previous pages!), but when I need a quick fix, this is my go-to.

4 tortilla wraps

1 quantity of essential pizza sauce (page 141), or 4 tsp tomato purée (paste) – see Notes

FOR A MARGHERITA TOPPING

40g (1½oz) low-fat mozzarella

7 cherry tomatoes

4–6 basil leaves

FOR A LEAN GREEN TOPPING

3 tenderstem broccoli, sliced in half lengthways

Handful of spinach (place in a colander and pour over boiling water to wilt, then squeeze out excess liquid)

6–8 pitted black olives, halved

50g (1¾oz) cottage cheese

1 tsp pesto

FOR AN EASY ONION TOPPING

½ red onion, finely sliced

30g (1oz) goat's cheese

1 thyme sprig, leaves picked

Drizzle of balsamic vinegar and some rocket (arugula), to finish

Preheat the oven to 240°C (220°C fan/475°F/gas 9).

Pop the tortilla wraps on a baking tray and spread 2 tablespoons of the tomato sauce over each, leaving a border for the crust. Next, top with your preferred toppings (use my suggestions or create your own), then bake for 6–8 minutes until the edge of your tortilla wraps are crisp and golden and any cheese has melted.

NOTES

If you want to really speed things up and don't have any pizza sauce, smooth on about 1 teaspoon of tomato purée (paste) straight from the tube onto each pizza!

Velvet Chicken Chow Mein

SERVES 4 · TAKES 50 MINUTES

I order the same thing every time I have a Chinese takeaway – prawn crackers, seaweed, chicken chow mein, special fried rice and sweet and sour pork balls. It's a lot for one human, but there's rarely an occasion where someone else in the room won't scoop up those last few noodles.

4 bundles of medium egg noodles (200g/7oz in total)

3 garlic cloves, crushed

5cm (2in) piece of fresh ginger, peeled and grated

2 tbsp light soy sauce

1 tbsp white wine vinegar

Pinch of sugar

1 tbsp vegetable oil

2 red (bell) peppers, deseeded and thinly sliced

½ savoy cabbage, thinly sliced (or 300g/10½oz beansprouts)

1 carrot, julienned

2 spring onions (scallions), chopped

Lime wedges, to serve

FOR THE VELVET CHICKEN

4 boneless, skinless chicken breasts

6 tbsp water

4 tsp light soy sauce

4 tsp cornflour (cornstarch)

1 tbsp vegetable oil

NOTES

Chow mein is a traditional Chinese dish made with egg noodles and stir-fried veggies. I love adding a protein, and my favourite is chicken, but you can try different meat, tofu or stick to veggies.

First I'm going to show you how to velvet chicken – an essential step in Chinese cooking that gives that familiar soft and tender texture to your takeaway chicken. Slice your chicken into equal slivers, 0.5–1cm (¼–½in) thick, slicing across the breast to help get the most tender meat. Add to a bowl with the water and soy and give it a good mix. Set aside for 5–10 minutes and you'll notice most of that water has been absorbed. Now add your cornflour and vegetable oil and stir to coat well. Set aside for another 15 minutes.

Fill a pan with boiling water and keep it on the boil. Blanch the chicken (in batches if necessary) until it's opaque, leave it for a few deep breaths more, then remove it from the water with a slotted spoon and transfer to a plate. This may all seem like a faff, but I promise it's worth it!

Fill the pan with clean water and bring to the boil, then cook the noodles according to the packet instructions. Drain and rinse thoroughly with cold water to avoid them clumping.

To make the sauce, mix the garlic, ginger, soy, vinegar and sugar together in a small bowl.

Now it's time to start cooking. This bit moves fast so make sure you have everything you need to hand. Place a wok or large frying pan over a high heat and, once hot, add the oil. Throw in your veggies and cook for 2–3 minutes until starting to catch colour and your cabbage is wilting. Then pour in the sauce and cook for 30 seconds.

Throw in your blanched chicken and cook for 30 seconds, moving it around the pan so it catches colour. Finish with your noodles and cook for 30 seconds, giving everything a good toss to combine.

Plate up with a squeeze of lime and dive in!

Pork and Pineapple Sweet and Sour

SERVES 4 · TAKES 25 MINUTES

Astonishingly vibrant orange but with a curious translucency... what is it? When it comes to takeaways, no matter how unidentifiable, I will always order sweet and sour. The sharp tang balanced by the vibrant sweetness; I can't get enough of it!

500g (1lb 2oz) pork fillet, cut into 3–4cm (1¼–1½in) chunks
1 x 435g (15oz) can of diced pineapple, in natural juice
4 tbsp tomato ketchup
3 tbsp white wine vinegar
2 garlic cloves, crushed
Thumb-sized piece of fresh ginger, peeled and grated
1 tsp vegetable oil
2 green (bell) peppers, deseeded and cut into chunks
1 tbsp cornflour (cornstarch)
2 tbsp water
Sliced spring onions, to serve

Put the pork in a bowl, add the juice from the can of pineapple (place the diced pineapple to one side), along with the ketchup, vinegar, garlic and ginger, and set aside for 10–15 minutes.

Meanwhile, heat the oil in a frying pan over a high heat, add the diced pineapple and the peppers and cook for 2–3 minutes. Give them a chance to catch before tossing or shaking them, as we want these to have a little bit of colour and caramelization.

Keep the heat relatively high and add the pork, reserving the marinade. Cook for 2–3 minutes so the pork starts to colour, then pour in the marinade and allow it to bubble with the pork and veggies.

Create a cornflour slurry by mixing the cornflour and water together, and add this to the pan, too. Whisk and cook for a further 2–3 minutes until the sauce is thick and glossy, then serve with some sliced spring onions on top.

Thai Green Curry Fried Rice

SERVES 4 · TAKES 20 MINUTES

Special fried rice is extra special in our household, as it's the one dish ordered and understood as 'the essential sharing dish'. It doesn't matter who suggested it, it's for the group and will be handed around the table – no permission required.

1 tsp vegetable oil

1 aubergine (eggplant), halved and sliced into 1cm (½in) thick half-moons

100g (3½oz) baby corn, halved lengthways

300g (10½oz) frozen peas

150g (5½oz) mangetout (snow peas)

5 tbsp Thai green curry paste

3 garlic cloves, crushed

2 x 250g (9oz) packets of microwavable rice

2 tbsp water

4 large free-range eggs

Fresh red or green chilli, sliced, to serve (optional)

Salt

Heat the oil in a large frying pan over a medium–high heat and add all the veggies and a generous pinch of salt. Cook for 8 minutes, getting a little colour on them, and then throw in the curry paste, garlic, rice and water and cook for a further 2–3 minutes until everything starts to soften.

Create 4 small wells in the vegetable rice and crack an egg into each one. Cover the pan and drop the heat to medium for 5–7 minutes.

You should end up with a slightly crispy bottom to your fried rice, tender vibrant veggies, and lightly steamed eggs. Serve into bowls, ensuring everyone gets an egg, and sprinkle with fresh chilli for added heat!

Stuffed Flatbreads 2 Ways

MAKES 8 · TAKES 45 MINUTES

At university, our local Indian restaurant – all hail 'King Babas' – would do a student special of £5 for main, rice and naan. It was a complete steal, topped off with a 'bring your own' policy for booze. Never did you feel more glorious than when you splashed out on a second stuffed bread to mop up the remaining curry.

I was taught how to make flatbreads by Chetna Makan in one of my first ever YouTube collaborations. I will be forever grateful for her time, talent and knowledge, not to mention her endlessly generous nature.

FOR THE FLATBREADS
100g (3½oz) wholemeal (wholewheat) flour, plus extra for dusting
70g (2¼oz) plain (all-purpose) flour
1½ tsp baking powder
¼ tsp fine salt
160g (5¾oz) plain yogurt

FOR THE PESHWARI-STYLE FILLING
2 tbsp coconut cream
50g (1¾oz) ground almonds
40g (1½oz) raisins
Pinch of salt

FOR THE KEEMA-STYLE FILLING
1 tsp vegetable oil
1 brown onion, finely chopped
3 garlic cloves, crushed
2.5cm (1in) piece of fresh ginger, peeled and grated
1 tbsp tomato paste
1 tsp chilli powder
1 tsp ground cumin
1 tsp garam masala
¼ tsp ground black pepper
1 tsp plain (all-purpose) flour
250g (9oz) lean minced (ground) turkey

If making Peshwari-style filling, mix the ingredients together into a paste and set aside.

If making keema-style filling, heat the oil in a large frying pan and soften the onion for 7–8 minutes. Throw in the garlic and ginger and cook for 1 minute before adding the tomato paste, ground spices and black pepper, cooking for another 2 minutes. Shake the flour evenly over the onion mixture and add the turkey mince. Fry for 4–5 minutes, so the turkey is coloured all the way through and your pan has no residual moisture. Set aside.

For the flatbreads, add both flours, the baking powder and salt to a mixing bowl and stir with a spoon. Add the yogurt and mix into a soft, slightly sticky dough.

Dust a clean work surface with flour, then tip out the dough. Knead for a minute or so to bring it all together (this isn't a traditional bread recipe, so you don't need to knead it for long – just enough time to bring everything together). Set aside to rest for 15 minutes so the flour can absorb the liquid, which makes the dough easier to handle.

Divide the dough into 8 equal pieces.

Roll the dough pieces into long rectangles, about 2mm (1/16in) thick. Spoon a portion of your chosen filling onto one half of the dough, spreading to form a thin layer. Fold the dough over to enclose the filling and press the edges together to seal. (If you're not filling your flatbreads, simply roll to a 5mm/¼in thickness.)

Place a griddle pan over a high heat and, once hot, cook each flatbread for 1–2 minutes on each side, or until lightly charred and puffed up.

NOTE

Wrap the flatbreads in a clean tea (dish) towel once cooked to keep them warm and soft.

Cheesy Root Veg Fries

SERVES 4 AS A SIDE · TAKES 30 MINUTES

A classic night out at uni would lead us to a club that had a burger van in the courtyard. In a bid to wrangle my newly single friend away from the lustful eyes of the hopeful and horny souls across the dance floor, I'd retreat to said burger van and order a sobering-sized portion of cheesy chips followed swiftly by a taxi home.

500g (1lb 2oz) root vegetables (potatoes, parsnips, carrots, beetroot/beet), cut into 1cm (½in) thick batons
2 tsp olive oil
Pinch of salt
50g (1¾oz) Parmesan, grated

Preheat the oven to 220°C (200°C fan/425°F/gas 7).

Add your prepared veggie batons to a bowl with the olive oil and salt, and toss to coat. It's personal preference as to whether you leave the skins on or not, but there's lots of goodness in the skins of root veggies so I encourage you to keep them on for added bite and nutrition!

Spread out in a single layer on a baking tray lined with baking paper and bake in the oven for 20–25 minutes, giving them a turn halfway through.

When your fries come out the oven, immediately sprinkle with the Parmesan. Wait for 5 minutes to allow the cheese to melt and set, then serve.

FRIDAY NIGHT IN

Katsu Curry Chicken Kyiv with Quick Pickled Salad

SERVES 4 · TAKES 1 HOUR 30 MINUTES

Clean slices of crispy chicken, sitting on a perfectly shaped mound of fluffy rice and drenched in a sweet, fragrant sauce. Those warm spices remind me of dark winter evenings being held up after work and ordering a delivery for when I finally made it home. I'd get stuck into it, tucked up on the sofa, gently discouraging the neighbour's cat from trying to sneak a piece off my plate.

4 boneless, skinless chicken breasts
8 tbsp panko breadcrumbs
4 tbsp ground almonds
1 large free-range egg, beaten
6 tbsp plain (all-purpose) flour
Salt and ground black pepper
Cooked fluffy rice, to serve

FOR THE KATSU SAUCE
1 large brown onion, finely chopped
3 garlic cloves, crushed
Thumb-sized piece of fresh ginger, peeled and grated
1 tbsp olive oil
4 tsp medium curry powder
½ tsp ground turmeric
2 tbsp plain (all-purpose) flour
100ml (3½fl oz/scant ½ cup) water

FOR THE QUICK PICKLED SALAD
1 carrot, ribboned (sliced lengthways with a swivel peeler)
1 cucumber, ribboned (sliced lengthways with a swivel peeler)
2 tbsp white wine vinegar
Pinch of salt
Pinch of sugar
½ tsp cumin seeds

For the sauce, place the onion, garlic, ginger and oil in a pan set over a gentle heat and soften for 10–12 minutes until everything turns translucent. Add the curry powder, turmeric and flour and cook for 2 minutes. Add the water and cook until you have a thick curry sauce. You can now blitz the sauce in a blender until smooth, or leave it chunky. Transfer to a piping (pastry) bag or sandwich bag and pop it in the fridge to cool and firm.

Slit a narrow but deep pocket into your chicken breasts by inserting a knife into the thickest end. Pipe a generous amount of katsu sauce inside. Place the filled chicken on a lined baking tray and into the freezer for 30 minutes.

Preheat the oven to 220°C (200°C fan/425°F/gas 7).

Combine the breadcrumbs and ground almonds in a bowl and season with salt and pepper. Add the beaten egg to a separate bowl and the flour to another. Pané (coat) your chicken, first in flour, then in the beaten egg, then in the seasoned breadcrumbs and almonds.

Pop the coated chicken back on the lined baking tray and bake for 25–30 minutes until cooked through and golden.

Meanwhile, combine all the ingredients for the quick pickled salad in a bowl and allow to sit for 15 minutes. Squeeze out any excess moisture before serving alongside the chicken and some fluffy rice.

Veg-packed Silky Tofu Ramen

SERVES 4 · TAKES 30 MINUTES

Most of these recipe intros feature boozy nights followed by filthy munchies, but we eat ramen most Fridays because it makes us feel so darn fantastic. It's full of flavour, colour, texture and good things, and is a doddle to throw together. One big bit of advice... buy some large bowls to serve it in.

4 large free-range eggs

4 bundles of rice noodles

200g (7oz) radishes, thinly sliced (ideally on a mandoline)

4 tbsp white wine vinegar

Pinch of salt

Sprinkle of sugar

1.2l (40fl oz/5 cups) vegetable stock

4 tbsp white miso paste

3 tsp fish sauce

200g (7oz) button (white) mushrooms

1 carrot, julienned

175g (6oz) baby corn, halved lengthways

½ sweetheart cabbage, shredded

4 sheets of sushi nori, plus extra to serve

280g (10oz) silken tofu

Boil the eggs in a large pan of simmering water for 7 minutes. For the last 3 minutes of cooking time, add the noodle bundles. When done, plunge the eggs and noodles into ice-cold water to stop the cooking process.

Pop the radishes into a bowl with the vinegar, salt and sugar. Give everything a good squeeze and then simply leave to pickle.

Grab an extra-large saucepan and add the stock, miso and fish sauce. Bring to a gentle simmer, then add the mushrooms and carrot and cover. Simmer for 5 minutes, then add the baby corn, cabbage and nori and cook for 2–3 minutes until softened.

Time to assemble. Divide the noodles between bowls then top with some silken tofu. Pour over the miso broth, ensuring each bowl gets some veggies. Peel then halve the boiled eggs, adding one to each bowl. Finally top with your pickled radishes and some extra nori, if you like.

FRIDAY NIGHT IN

Black Bean Dhal

SERVES 2–4 (SEE NOTE) · TAKES 1 HOUR

One of my favourite things about living in London is being able to experience so many cultural cuisines on our doorstep. My husband actually remembers the first time I tasted dhal – I spent a good hour describing its rich, creamy, smoky, luxurious flavours in relentless detail. It's safe to say I was hooked.

190g (6¾oz) dried red lentils
1 tsp olive oil
1 brown onion, chopped
2 garlic cloves, crushed
1 tsp ground cumin
1 tsp ground coriander
1 tsp ground turmeric
1 tsp paprika
700ml (24fl oz/3 cups) vegetable stock
1 x 400g (14oz) can of black beans, drained and rinsed
Salt and ground black pepper

TO FINISH
Finely chopped coriander (cilantro)
Low-fat plain yogurt

Rinse the lentils in cold water and set aside.

Heat the oil in a large saucepan over a medium–high heat. Add the onion and garlic and sauté for 10 minutes until the onion is translucent. Add the cumin, coriander, turmeric and paprika and stir to combine.

Add the rinsed lentils to the pan and stir to coat them in the spices. Pour in the vegetable stock and bring to a boil.

Reduce the heat to low and simmer for 20–25 minutes, stirring occasionally, until the lentils are tender and fully cooked.

Add the black beans to the pan and stir gently to combine. Season with salt and pepper to taste, then simmer for a further 5–10 minutes until heated through, thick and creamy.

Sprinkle over some coriander and dollops of yogurt before serving.

NOTE

This serves 2 people for supper or 4 people as part of a larger spread. Try serving it alongside my chickpea and coconut curry (page 100), stuffed flatbreads (page 151) or poppadom nachos (page 137) for a proper Friday night feast.

Beef Rendang Kebabs

SERVES 4 · TAKES 30 MINUTES

In my home town of Wokingham there used to be a kebab van parked up on the main road, and I'm certain the owners retired to a mansion, as they were never without a crowd thronging around them. The spits dripped juices that were joyfully soaked up by the fluffy flatbreads that they stuffed full of vibrant pickles and lashings of garlic mayonnaise.

500g (1lb 2oz) lean minced (ground) beef
1 small brown onion, grated
2 garlic cloves, crushed
1 tsp ground turmeric
1 tsp ground cumin
1 tsp ground coriander
½ tsp ground ginger
½ tsp salt
¼ tsp ground black pepper
Flatbreads (see page 151 for homemade), to serve
Herby salad, to serve

FOR THE RENDANG SAUCE
1 tbsp vegetable oil
1 small brown onion, finely chopped
2 garlic cloves, crushed
1 red chilli, finely chopped
1 lemongrass stalk, bruised and finely chopped
1 tsp ground turmeric
1½ tsp ground cumin
1 tsp ground coriander
1½ tbsp plain (all-purpose) flour
400ml (14fl oz/1¾ cups) light coconut milk
2 tsp white wine vinegar
½ vegetable stock cube

In a large bowl, mix together the beef, grated onion, garlic, ground spices, salt and pepper until well combined.

Divide the mixture into 8 equal portions and press each around a skewer to form a sausage shape.

Heat a frying pan (or ideally griddle pan) over a medium–high heat and cook the kebabs for about 8 minutes on each side or until cooked through. You can also do this on the BBQ (grill).

While the kebabs are cooking, make the sauce by heating the vegetable oil in a saucepan over a medium heat. Add the onion, garlic, chilli and lemongrass and cook for 2–3 minutes until softened. Add the turmeric, cumin, coriander and plain flour and cook for another 2–3 minutes until fragrant and the flour has been integrated.

Pour in the coconut milk and white wine vinegar and crumble in the stock cube, then bring to a simmer. Reduce the heat to low and let the sauce simmer for about 10 minutes, stirring occasionally, until it has thickened and the stock cube has dissolved. Season generously.

Serve the kebabs stuffed into flatbreads with a herby salad and the rendang sauce drizzled over.

FRIDAY NIGHT IN

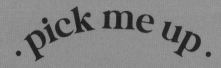

Perfectly Popped Popcorn 4 Ways

SERVES 4 · TAKES 20 MINUTES

It's 1997 and we've been taken to see *Men in Black* at the cinema. I'm six years too young for the rating, but it's the '90s and no one cares. It's an early scene where the alien steals the farmer's skin and my excitement at being at the cinema turns to terrified crying. Dad shuffles me out of the screening and consoles me with my very own bag of freshly popped popcorn. A necessary comfort food turned into a wonderful memory.

80g (2¾oz) corn kernels (20g/¾oz per person)

NOTES

Treat yourself to a new bag of kernels. Kernels contain water that expands the soft, starchy inside as you heat them, until eventually they pop. The older your kernels, the less likely they are to pop and the less fluffy your popcorn!

Popcorn when just popped (before the flavours are added) can be happily stored in an airtight container in a cool dry place for one week (if you think you can last that long).

ON-THE-STOVE POPCORN

Start by putting a non-stick pan (that has a tight-fitting lid) on the stove. You want your pan to heat up to a toasty temperature, but we don't want our kernels to burn. The best way to test is to drop a touch of water into the pan. If it reacts by angrily sizzling and steaming, turn your temperature down. If it lightly fizzes, we're ready to rock and roll.

Add the kernels and immediately put the lid on. Keep shaking the pan every few seconds and in just a few minutes it should start popping! Keep going until there's a delay of a few seconds between the last few pops.

MICROWAVE POPCORN

Pop the kernels into a lidded, microwave-friendly pot (this can also work with a microwave-safe bowl and snug-fitting plate). Microwave on your highest setting and listen out for the pops! Once your pops have slowed to one every few seconds, take it out so you don't burn your gorgeously fluffed snacks.

By all means season with the classics of salt and/or sugar, but I want to show you some fun ways to jazz up your perfectly popped popcorn...

TOP BANANAS

30g (1oz) dried banana chips
30g (1oz) walnuts
1 tbsp unsweetened cocoa powder
1 tsp ground cinnamon

Add the ingredients to a blender and blitz into a powder. Sprinkle it over your freshly popped popcorn, giving it a good shake to make sure it's evenly coated, then tuck in. If you want it any sweeter, add 1 tablespoon of runny honey to your hot popcorn. This will also help your coating stick.

TRAIL MIX

40g (1½oz) cranberries
40g (1½oz) pumpkin seeds
3 tbsp almond butter (or peanut butter)
2 tbsp honey
60g (2¼oz) ground almonds

Mix your cranberries and pumpkin seeds together with the freshly popped popcorn. Mix your almond butter and honey in a bowl and warm in the microwave on short 10-second blasts to make it runny, then drizzle over the popcorn. Mix everything well, then grab a handful of popcorn mix and press and roll it into a sticky ball. Add the ground almonds to a separate bowl, then roll each ball in it to coat. Pop the coated popcorn balls onto a baking tray and stick them the fridge for a little while to firm up before enjoying.

ROAST DINNER

1 chicken stock cube (ideally OXO because it
    crumbles well)
5 thyme sprigs
1 tsp garlic granules

Add the ingredients to a pestle and mortar or a blender and pulse into a powder. Sprinkle over your freshly popped popcorn, giving it a good shake to make sure it's evenly coated, then tuck in.

LET'S GET SPICY

1 tsp chilli powder
Zest of 1 lemon
80g finely grated Parmesan or pecorino

Sprinkle the ingredients over your freshly popped popcorn, giving it a good shake to make sure it's evenly coated, then tuck in.

Sundays

Sundays have always been my favourite day
of the week. That steaming cup of tea after
standing in the freezing cold watching my
brother play football was a joy, and things only
got better from there, because we all knew
what came next: The Roast.

Whether beef, lamb, pork or chicken, one thing
was always certain – we'd all eat too much, slob
out on the sofa with a film and fall asleep.

This chapter is your ultimate guide to the
perfect Sunday roast to share with the people
who really matter. Tweaked to give you the
ideal level of satisfaction and just enough food
lethargy to let you know you've done Sunday
right, but that Monday won't be a trudge.

A Perfectly
Roasted Chicken

SERVES 4 · TAKES 1 HOUR 20 MINUTES

Every photo of me as a child features food, and most often it would be a chicken drumstick. A delicious pacifier that would guarantee to keep me quiet for at least 20 minutes.

1 lemon, halved
1 free-range chicken (about 1.6kg/3½lb)
1 whole garlic bulb, halved horizontally
Bunch of fresh thyme
2 tbsp olive oil
Salt and ground black pepper

Preheat the oven to 240°C (220°C fan/475°F/gas 9).

Squeeze the lemon halves over the chicken. Place the garlic bulb halves inside the chicken along with the thyme and the squeezed lemon halves.

Rub the olive oil all over the chicken and season generously with salt and pepper.

Place the chicken in a roasting tray, breast side up. Roast for 15 minutes, then drop the temperature to 210°C (190°C fan/410°F/gas 6–7) and continue to roast for another 45 minutes or until a meat thermometer inserted into the thickest part of the thigh reads 74°C (165°F), or the juices in the thickest part of the thigh run clear.

Remove the chicken from the oven and let it rest for 10 minutes before carving.

NOTES

For any meal at home we opt for a whole chicken rather than buying just the breasts or thighs because it's more cost-effective (more meat for your money). It gives versatility to your meal planning (you can plan to cook one night with the chicken breast and another night with the wings etc.). And finally, there's more flavour and moisture in a whole chicken.

Turn your leftover chicken carcass into chicken stock by simmering it in water with vegetables and herbs for several hours, then strain the liquid and discard the solids. That liquid will be a richly flavoured stock.

Paprika Roasted
Baby Potatoes

SERVES 4 · TAKES 1 HOUR

I will fight you for the flattest, crunchiest roast potato in the pan. I want a fluffy centre, but I mostly want that salty snap. It feels as though you could make a roast potato any day of the week, but on a Sunday (or Christmas) they herald a whole new level of sublimeness.

750g (1lb 10½oz) baby potatoes, halved
2 tbsp olive oil
1 tsp garlic granules
1 tsp smoked paprika
1 tsp dried thyme
1 tsp salt
½ tsp ground black pepper
2 tbsp grated Parmesan

Preheat the oven to 240°C (220°C fan/475°F/gas 9).

Place the halved baby potatoes in a large bowl. Add the olive oil, garlic granules, smoked paprika, dried thyme, salt and pepper, and toss well to coat the potatoes evenly.

Line a baking tray with baking paper and spread the potatoes out in a single layer. Bake for 45–50 minutes or until crispy and golden brown.

Sprinkle the grated Parmesan over the potatoes and bake for an additional 5 minutes or until the cheese is melted and bubbly.

Serve immediately as a side dish for your roast dinner.

Pictured on page 167.

NOTES

Baby potatoes have a thin and delicate skin that does not need to be peeled, making them easier and quicker to prepare. This also means that the nutrients found in the skin are retained, providing more nutritional value.

Mustard and Maple Glazed Carrots

SERVES 4 · TAKES 45 MINUTES

Carrots are the unsung hero of a roast dinner. We celebrate the spud, the meats and the Yorkshire puddings, but when a carrot glistens with a salty honey glaze and cuts like butter, I am captivated.

500g (1lb 2oz) baby carrots, peeled
2 tbsp olive oil
¼ tsp salt
¼ tsp ground black pepper
2 tbsp maple syrup
1 tbsp Dijon mustard
½ tsp garlic granules

Preheat the oven to 200°C (180°C fan/400°F/gas 6).

In a large bowl, toss the baby carrots with the olive oil, salt and pepper. Spread out in a single layer on a baking tray and roast in the oven for about 40 minutes or until tender.

While the carrots are roasting, mix the maple syrup, mustard and garlic granules in a small bowl. When the carrots are done roasting, remove them from the oven and drizzle the glaze over them.

Return the tray to the oven and roast for an additional 5 minutes, or until the glaze is bubbly and caramelized.

Pictured on page 167.

Pork Stuffing Meatloaf

SERVES 4 · TAKES 1 HOUR 20 MINUTES

My brother-in-law is an exceptional cook and can knock up a roast dinner worthy of a Michelin star. I always ensure I'm wearing an elasticated waistband when we get the golden-ticket invite to a Sunday roast there. His incredible understanding of the humblest cuts of meat has inspired this dish. I may even cook it for him one day.

1 tbsp olive oil, plus extra for greasing

1 leek, finely sliced

50g (1¾oz) wholemeal (wholewheat) breadcrumbs

120ml (4fl oz/½ cup) skimmed milk (or dairy-free alternative)

1 large free-range egg

½ brown onion, finely chopped

1 garlic clove, crushed

1 tbsp dried oregano

500g (1lb 2oz) lean minced (ground) pork

Salt and ground black pepper

Preheat the oven to 160°C (140°C fan/325°F/gas 3).

Heat the olive oil in a pan set over a medium heat, then add the leek, 1 tablespoon of water and a pinch of salt. Cook and sweat for 5 minutes until softened.

In a bowl, mix the breadcrumbs and milk until the breadcrumbs are fully saturated. Add the egg, onion, garlic and oregano, and season with salt and pepper. Mix well.

Add the pork mince and softened leeks to the bowl and mix until the meat and leeks are evenly incorporated into the breadcrumb mixture.

Grease a 450g (1lb) loaf pan with olive oil and transfer the meat mixture into it, packing it down firmly.

Bake for at least 1 hour or until the internal temperature of the meatloaf reaches 70°C (158°F) on a cooking thermometer. If you don't have a thermometer, insert a fork or metal skewer into the centre and check it is hot all the way through.

Let it rest for about 10 minutes, then invert onto a board before slicing and serving.

Optional step: before serving, sear each side of the meatloaf for 2–3 minutes in a frying pan set over a medium–high heat. This will add some lovely colour.

Sticky Roasted Parsnip and Apple Salad

SERVES 4 · TAKES 35 MINUTES

It doesn't matter what dinner we're eating, Nanny and Grandpa will always serve it with a salad. This may not be a leafy green one, but finishing off your roasted veggies with a salad dressing adds a stunning whack of flavour!

4 large parsnips, peeled and cut into thin wedges
2 medium dessert apples, cored and cut into thin wedges
2 tbsp olive oil
30g (1oz) walnuts, chopped
2 tbsp honey
2 tbsp apple cider vinegar
1 tsp Dijon mustard
30g (1oz) feta, crumbled
Small handful of parsley leaves, roughly chopped
Salt and ground black pepper

Preheat the oven to 220°C (200°C fan/425°F/gas 7).

In a large bowl, toss the parsnips and apples with the olive oil and a sprinkle of salt and pepper. Spread the parsnips and apples in a single layer on a baking tray and roast for 25–30 minutes, or until tender and lightly browned.

Toast the walnuts in a dry frying pan over a medium heat for 3–4 minutes, or until fragrant.

In a small bowl, whisk together the honey, apple cider vinegar and mustard, and season with salt and pepper.

Time to assemble. Combine your roasted parsnips and apples with the toasted walnuts and honey vinaigrette, then top with the crumbled feta and parsley to serve.

Pictured on page 170.

Slow-roasted Red Cabbage and Shallots

SERVES 4 · TAKES 1 HOUR 45 MINUTES

Red cabbage has become essential to any Sunday when my sister-in-law is present. Staining the rest of her dinner vibrant purple, it is over 50% of her serving. Saucy with a slight snap, sweetly spiced and steaming, it really is a brightener to any roast dinner.

1 large red cabbage, finely shredded
2 tbsp olive oil
2 tbsp balsamic vinegar
1 tbsp honey
1 tsp ground cinnamon
4 shallots, sliced
Salt and ground black pepper

Preheat the oven to 180°C (160°C fan/350°F/gas 4).

In a large bowl, mix the shredded red cabbage, olive oil, vinegar, honey, cinnamon and a pinch of salt and pepper until well combined. Transfer the mixture to a large roasting dish.

Scatter the sliced shallots over the top of the cabbage mixture. Cover the roasting dish with foil and cook in the oven for 1 hour and 30 minutes or until the cabbage is tender and the shallots are caramelized.

Once done, remove from the oven and serve hot (though it's also a delicious little treat in a cheese sandwich the next day!).

Pictured on page 175.

Moreish Mushroom and Walnut Loaf

SERVES 4 · TAKES 1 HOUR

I'm not sure I've ever shared a veggie loaf with my grandparents. They are from the meat-and-two-veg era, and a vegetarian centrepiece would seem like an overinflated stuffing. But this is a real showstopper. A glossy, moist, gluttonous veggie loaf that even Grandpa Gordon would be sold on.

1 tbsp olive oil, plus extra for greasing

1 brown onion, finely chopped

1 celery stick, finely chopped

70g (2½oz) mushrooms, finely chopped

120g (4¼oz) walnuts, chopped

100g (3½oz) pecans, chopped

1 carrot, grated

60g (2¼oz) wholemeal (wholewheat) breadcrumbs

30g (1oz) plain (all-purpose) flour

2 tbsp tomato paste

2 tbsp light soy sauce

6 thyme sprigs, leaves only (about 1 tbsp)

3 rosemary sprigs, leaves only (about 1 tbsp)

Salt and ground black pepper

Preheat the oven to 210°C (190°C fan/410°F/gas 6–7).

Heat the oil in a large frying pan over a medium heat. Add the onion and celery and cook until softened, then add the mushrooms and cook until they release their moisture and become tender.

In a large mixing bowl, combine the chopped walnuts and pecans, grated carrot, breadcrumbs, flour, tomato paste, soy sauce, thyme, rosemary, and a pinch each of salt and pepper.

Add the cooked vegetables to the mixing bowl and stir until well combined.

Grease a 450g (1lb) loaf pan with olive oil, then transfer the mixture to the tin and press down firmly.

Bake for 35–40 minutes or until golden brown on top. Let cool for a few minutes, then invert onto a board before slicing and serving.

NOTES

The nut roast will keep in the fridge for up to 4 days, tightly wrapped in cling film (plastic wrap) or foil. Wrap and place in an airtight container to freeze it for up to 3 months.

To reheat, remove the nut roast from the fridge or freezer and let it sit at room temperature for 30 minutes, while you preheat the oven to 210°C (190°C fan/410°F/gas 6–7). Place the nut roast on a baking tray and cover it with foil. Bake for 20 minutes if reheating from the fridge or 40 minutes if reheating from frozen.

Roasted Squash with Quinoa Stuffing

SERVES 4 · TAKES 1 HOUR 10 MINUTES

My Liverpool aunties are ridiculously creative both in crafts and in the kitchen. With a few fussy eaters in the family and a couple of complicated diets, this is where their imaginative prowess comes into its own. Why shouldn't a veggie dish become the centrepiece?

1 medium butternut squash, halved lengthways and deseeded
2 tbsp olive oil, plus extra for brushing
90g (3¼oz) quinoa
500ml (17fl oz/2 cups) vegetable stock
60g (2¼oz) baby spinach, chopped
60g (2¼oz) pecans, chopped
40g (1½oz) dried cranberries
30g (1oz) feta, crumbled
Salt and ground black pepper

Preheat the oven to 220°C (200°C fan/425°F/gas 7).

Brush the inside of the squash halves with olive oil and sprinkle with salt and pepper. Place cut side down on a baking tray and roast for 40–45 minutes, or until tender.

While the squash is roasting, rinse the quinoa and add it to a saucepan with the vegetable stock. Bring to a boil over a high heat, then reduce the heat to low and simmer for 15–20 minutes, or until all the liquid has been absorbed.

In a large mixing bowl, combine the cooked quinoa, baby spinach, pecans, dried cranberries, feta and the 2 tablespoons of olive oil, and season with salt and pepper.

Once the squash is done roasting, remove it from the oven and let it cool for a few minutes. Turn the halves over and stuff each with the quinoa mixture. Return the stuffed squash to the oven and roast for an additional 10–15 minutes, or until everything is heated through. I love to serve this with a drizzle of herby mint sauce (page 186).

NOTES

Did you know, you can plant your discarded squash seeds? Choose a sunny location with well-draining soil and plant the seeds in late spring after the last frost, about 2.5cm (1in) deep and 60–90cm (2–3 feet) apart, watering regularly.

Cauliflower and Cashew Cheese

SERVES 4 · TAKES 2 HOURS 30 MINUTES

I think it's impossible for my auntie to serve a roast dinner without at least seven vegetable side dishes. Cauliflower cheese is always one of them – drowning in a creamy, unctuous cheddar sauce that I can smother across the rest of my dinner.

1 cauliflower, cut into florets (discard the stalk)

120g (4¼oz) cashews, soaked in water for at least 2 hours

300ml (11fl oz/1¼ cups) skimmed milk (or dairy-free alternative)

1 tbsp white miso paste

1½ tsp garlic granules

1½ tsp onion granules

1 tsp cornflour (cornstarch)

80g (2¾oz) Cheddar, grated

Handful of parsley, finely chopped (optional)

Salt and ground black pepper

Preheat the oven to 200°C (180°C fan/400°F/gas 6).

Blanch the cauliflower florets in boiling salted water until tender, about 7–10 minutes.

Drain the soaked cashews and add them to a blender or food processor along with the milk, miso paste, garlic granules, onion granules, cornflour, two-thirds of your grated cheddar and a generous pinch of salt and pepper. Blend until smooth and creamy.

In a large bowl, combine the steamed cauliflower with the cashew sauce, and mix well. Transfer the mixture to a baking dish, sprinkle with the remaining grated Cheddar and bake for 20–25 minutes until bubbly and golden brown on top.

Sprinkle with some chopped parsley, if you like, and serve.

NOTES

I appreciate soaking cashews is a bit of a pain but doing so will give you an even creamier cheese sauce and it improves their nutritional value (as it does with most nuts!).

You can switch out the cauliflower for other vegetables. Broccoli and leeks work well.

Store-cupboard Gravy

MAKES 250ML (9FL OZ/1 CUP) · TAKES 20 MINUTES

You're either greedy with gravy or it brings out the social etiquette side of you. Personally, I fall into the former camp, but am too ashamed to go the whole way. My technique: Step 1 – pour on lashings of gravy until your plate resembles a stew. Then, once you reach the rationing stage, it's time for the dance of Step 2 – trying to politely not take the last drop, but taking as much as I can while leaving a teaspoon or so remaining in the jug to avoid recrimination.

Sometimes you just need gravy, and if you've not got the juices from a dripping meat joint, or you don't want to settle for gravy granules, here's an easy and quick little store-cupboard gravy.

1 tbsp olive oil
1 tbsp plain (all-purpose) flour
1 tsp tomato paste
1 tsp Marmite
350ml (12fl oz/1½ cups) chicken or vegetable stock
½ tsp garlic granules
½ tsp onion granules
1 tsp white wine vinegar (optional)
Salt and ground black pepper

Heat the oil in a small saucepan over a medium heat. Add the flour and whisk constantly for 2–3 minutes until it turns golden brown. Beat in the tomato paste and Marmite, then slowly pour in the stock while continuously whisking to prevent lumps from forming.

Add the garlic granules, onion granules, white wine vinegar (optional) and salt and pepper to taste. Bring the mixture to a boil, then reduce the heat and let it simmer for 5–10 minutes until it thickens to your desired consistency. The longer you cook it, the darker the colour becomes.

Remove from the heat and serve hot over your roast dinner.

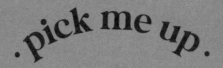

· pick me up ·

Simple Scrap Crisps

SERVES 4 · TAKES 10–15 MINUTES

The family allotment is one of my happy places. We spent a summer transforming it from a pile of mud to a well-organized retreat with raised wooden beds blossoming with potatoes, corn, raspberries and rhubarb. When you've grown something from seed, it's hard to see any of it wasted, so we found a way to put our scraps to good use, too!

You can make this recipe using vegetable peelings, or with whole unpeeled vegetables that have been very thinly sliced.

300g (10½oz) root vegetable peelings OR root vegetables very thinly sliced with a mandoline or vegetable peeler (I like to use a mixture of carrot, parsnip, potato and beetroot/beet)

2 tbsp olive oil

Salt and ground black pepper

SUGGESTED SEASONINGS

Potatoes: garlic granules and dried sage

Carrots: ground ginger and cumin

Beetroot: ground cinnamon and dried thyme

Sweet potatoes: ground nutmeg and cinnamon

Preheat the oven to 200°C (180°C fan/400°F/gas 6).

Sandwich your vegetables peelings or slices between a few sheets of kitchen paper to remove any excess moisture, then toss in a bowl with the oil and some salt and pepper.

Add your chosen seasonings and toss again. (Add no more than 1½ teaspoons of additional seasoning for every 300g/10½oz of veg; e.g. ½ teaspoon of dried sage and 1 teaspoon of garlic granules.)

Spread the seasoned vegetables in a single layer on a non-stick baking tray and bake for 10 minutes. Or (even better) stick them in an air-fryer for 4–5 minutes.

Veggie-stuffed
Yorkshire Pudding Pies

SERVES 4 · TAKES 1 HOUR 20 MINUTES

I've always been someone who plays with their food. Mashed potato gets sculpted into various shapes, patterns wiggled into gravy, and the Yorkshire pudding becomes a vehicle for everything else on my plate. So obviously I had to play with the classic pud and make it even more comforting.

125g (4½oz) plain (all-purpose) flour
½ tsp salt
½ tsp baking powder
2 large free-range eggs
240ml (8fl oz/1 cup) skimmed milk
    (or dairy-free alternative)
2 tbsp olive oil, plus 1 tsp for the veg
1 brown onion, finely chopped
2 garlic cloves, crushed
1 carrot, chopped
1 courgette (zucchini), chopped
75g (2½oz) frozen peas
Salt and ground black pepper

In a large bowl, mix the flour, salt and baking powder. In another bowl, whisk together the eggs and milk. Add the wet ingredients to the dry ingredients and mix until smooth. Cover the bowl and refrigerate for at least 30 minutes.

Preheat the oven to 200°C (180°C fan/400°F/ gas 6). Add the 2 tablespoons of olive oil to a 23cm (9in) pie dish and place it in the oven to get nice and hot.

Heat a frying pan over a medium heat with the 1 teaspoon of oil. Add the onion, garlic, carrot and courgette and cook for 10–12 minutes until tender. Add the frozen peas and cook for another minute. Give everything a generous season with salt and pepper.

Working quickly and carefully, tip the vegetable mixture into the hot pie dish, followed by the batter. Place in the oven and bake for 40–50 minutes, or until the pudding is golden brown and puffed up. Serve hot and enjoy!

NOTES

You can make regular Yorkshire puddings with this batter – simply pour the batter into a hot muffin tray (with each pocket filled with a drizzle of hot oil). Cook in the oven for 20–25 minutes.

Have you ever tried a sweet Yorkshire pudding? Cook the batter without the veggies and serve with ice cream and a drizzle of maple syrup. Absolutely delicious.

Double Potato Dauphinoise

SERVES 4 · TAKES 1 HOUR 40 MINUTES

One of my first 'fine dining' experiences was at a classic French restaurant and they served gratin dauphinoise. Wafer-thin potatoes placed meticulously in a small ramekin and bubbling with milk and cheese. I can still taste it now.

2 large sweet potatoes

3 large white potatoes

225ml (7¾fl oz/scant 1 cup) semi-skimmed milk (or dairy-free alternative)

200ml (7fl oz/scant 1 cup) vegetable stock

3 garlic cloves, crushed

1 tsp dried thyme

Olive oil, for greasing

30g (1oz) Parmesan, grated

Salt and ground black pepper

Handful of parsley leaves, finely chopped, to serve (optional)

Preheat the oven to 200°C (180°C fan/400°F/gas 6).

Peel the sweet potatoes and white potatoes. Dice one of the white potatoes into small cubes, then slice the remaining sweet potatoes and white potatoes into 5mm (¼in) discs (I like using a mandoline) and set aside.

In a small saucepan set over a medium heat, warm the milk, vegetable stock, garlic and thyme, with a good pinch of salt and a sprinkle of pepper. Add the diced potato and bring to a simmer. When the potato is very soft, mash and beat the mixture to a smooth purée (alternatively, purée in a blender or food processor). The sauce should be the consistency of cream – if not, add a splash of milk to loosen.

Lightly oil a 20cm (8in) square baking dish and layer the potato slices in the dish, slightly overlapping each other. Pour the sauce over the potatoes, cover the dish with foil and bake for 45–50 minutes.

Remove the foil, sprinkle the Parmesan on top of the potatoes and bake, uncovered, for an additional 15 minutes or until the cheese is melted and bubbly.

Garnish with chopped parsley before serving, if you like.

Herby Mint Sauce

MAKES 1 JAR · TAKES 5 MINUTES

We have such an absurdly large condiment selection that it takes up two shelves of our fridge because we can't resist a dollop of something extra on our dish. And I'm not necessarily committed to the classics. Have you ever tried mayonnaise spiked with mustard on your roast chicken? But there's no denying that mint jelly and cranberry sauce were created to dazzle our final dishes with their gemstone ruby and emerald colours.

2 tbsp honey
2 tbsp apple cider vinegar
30g (1oz) mint leaves, finely chopped
10g (⅓oz) parsley leaves, finely chopped
10g (⅓oz) coriander (cilantro) leaves, finely chopped
2 tbsp olive oil
Salt and ground black pepper

In a small bowl, whisk together the honey and vinegar until well combined. Add in the chopped herbs, then slowly pour in the olive oil, whisking continuously.

Season with salt and pepper to taste and serve.

NOTES

Homemade mint sauce can be stored in the fridge for up to 2 weeks. It is important to keep it in an airtight container or jar to maintain freshness. If the mint sauce appears to have changed colour, texture or smell, it should be discarded.

To freeze, simply pour the sauce into an ice-cube tray and freeze. Once frozen, transfer the cubes to a freezer bag and store in the freezer for up to 3 months. Thaw by transferring the desired number of cubes to the fridge overnight.

Orange and Cranberry Sauce

MAKES 1 JAR · TAKES 20 MINUTES

I was convinced cranberry sauce was exclusively for Christmas – that is until my friend asked if we had a jar during our Sunday roast and I realized this lip-smacking fruity delight deserves a year-round pass. If you've ever contemplated making it for a roast dinner, I guarantee you won't regret giving it a whirl.

100g (3½oz) fresh cranberries
120ml (4fl oz/½ cup) unsweetened apple sauce (you can find this in the baby-food aisle!)
60ml (2fl oz/¼ cup) orange juice
1 tbsp honey
¼ tsp ground cinnamon
Tiny pinch of freshly grated nutmeg

Rinse the cranberries and place them in a medium saucepan. Add the remaining ingredients and stir until well combined.

Bring the mixture to the boil over a medium heat, stirring occasionally. Reduce the heat to low and simmer for 10–15 minutes or until the cranberries have burst and the sauce has thickened.

Remove from the heat and let cool for a few minutes before serving.

NOTES

Homemade cranberry sauce can be stored in the fridge for up to 2 weeks. It's important to keep it in an airtight container or jar to maintain freshness. If the sauce appears to have changed colour, texture or smell, it should be discarded.

To freeze, simply pour the sauce into an ice-cube tray and freeze. Once frozen, transfer the cubes to a freezer bag and store in the freezer for up to 3 months. Thaw by transferring the desired number of cubes to the fridge overnight.

Just Desserts

Mum has mastered every feasible birthday cake over the years. From Postman Pat's van and an adorable Peter Rabbit cake when we were children, to the much more complicated requests of her grandsons today, baking is her forte.

And it's not surprising, as Mum has the sweetest tooth I have ever known; you can't get in her car without sitting on a packet of fruit gums. Sweet treats are most people's ultimate comfort food. The sugar rush that reminds us of being children and being told our teeth with fall out.

This chapter is filled with delights and clever creations that let you feel indulgent as you round off your meal – without wrecking it.

Tahini Flapjack, Date Caramel and Dark Chocolate Millionaires

MAKES 12 SQUARES · TAKES 1 HOUR

I'm from the school dinners era of sponge cake drenched in icing and sprinkles, honey sandwiches and Angel Delight, and NOTHING pleased me more than when I got to the dessert part of the canteen carousel to find a square of millionaire's shortbread in a little half-paper-half-plastic bag twisted closed. A crumbly biscuit layer, drenched in sweet, sticky caramel with a snap of chocolate on top – this really is the richest biscuit ever created and I can't wait for you to try my sneakily virtuous version.

FOR LAYER 1: THE 'FLAPJACK'
2 tbsp coconut oil, plus extra for greasing
3 tbsp tahini
60g (2¼oz) runny honey
2 ripe bananas
45g (1½oz) mixed seeds
150g (5½oz) rolled (porridge) oats

FOR LAYER 2: THE 'CARAMEL'
300g (10½oz) pitted dates
2 tbsp peanut butter
Pinch of salt

FOR LAYER 3: THE CHOCOLATE
200g (7oz) dark (semisweet) chocolate
   (minimum 70% cocoa solids)

Preheat the oven to 220°C (200°C fan/425°F/gas 7). Grease a deep, 20cm (8in) square baking pan.

Melt the coconut oil in a saucepan, then stir in the tahini and honey. Mash your bananas up and work them into the mix, then add your seeds and oats.

Tip your 'flapjack' mixture into your greased baking tray and press and flatten the mixture firmly, being sure to push it into the corners. Bake in the oven for 20 minutes.

For the 'caramel', if your dates are a bit dry, revive them in hot water for 15 minutes and then drain away the water before adding them to a food processor with the peanut butter and salt. Pulse until a tacky caramel-like dough forms. If it needs loosening you can add 1 teaspoon of warm water at a time. You want it runny enough that it will spread but not so runny that it won't hold its shape and set.

Once your 'flapjack' has cooled, pour over the 'caramel' and pop in the fridge to set.

Melt your dark chocolate either in a heatproof bowl set over a pan of simmering water, making sure the base of the bowl isn't touching the water, or in short 10-second blasts in the microwave. Pour the chocolate over your cooled caramel and return to the fridge to set.

Cut into squares and serve with a nice cup of tea!

NOTES

Best stored in an airtight container for 1 week in the fridge, or up to 3 months in the freezer.

Baked Strawberry Doughnuts

MAKES 8 LARGE DOUGHNUTS · TAKES 3 HOURS

Doughnuts are my biggest craving. I can't even entertain the concept of walking past a doughnut shop without at least enquiring about their latest flavours. But I don't need my doughnuts stuffed with six different types of chocolate and garnished with an edible theme park. I am a sucker for a classic jam-filled bun!

FOR THE DOUGH
170ml (6fl oz/scant ¾ cup) skimmed milk
15g (½oz) unsalted butter
7g (2 tsp) fast-action dried yeast
200g (7oz) plain (all-purpose) flour,
    plus extra for dusting
25g (1oz) instant mashed potato flakes
1 tsp granulated or caster (superfine) sugar
½ tsp baking powder
½ tsp fine salt
1 medium free-range egg
Vegetable oil, for greasing

FOR THE JAM (JELLY) FILLING
350g (12oz) fresh strawberries, hulled and
    roughly chopped
1 tbsp runny honey
1 tbsp lemon juice

TO COAT
30g (1oz) unsalted butter, melted
60g (2¼oz) granulated or caster (superfine) sugar

Firstly, make the dough. Add the milk and butter to a small saucepan, place over a low heat and warm until the butter is almost fully melted. Remove from the heat and set aside so the butter can finish melting and the milk cools to lukewarm. Once the mixture is lukewarm, stir in the yeast. Set aside for 5 minutes.

In the bowl of a stand mixer fitted with the dough hook, combine the flour, potato flakes, sugar, baking powder and salt. Stir together briefly to combine.

Pour the milk and yeast mixture into the bowl with the flour mixture, then add the egg. Mix on a slow speed to get a rough dough, then leave to rest for 15 minutes (this lets the flour properly absorb the liquids). Turn the mixer on to a medium speed for 10–15 minutes until the dough is stretchy, smooth, and pulling away from the sides of the bowl.

Drizzle a small amount of oil over the dough and scrape down the sides of the bowl, flipping the dough over so it's coated. Cover with a damp tea (dish) towel and set aside somewhere warm for around 30–45 minutes, until doubled in volume. You can tell when the dough is ready by using the 'poke test' – gently poke the dough with your fingertip, an impression should be left that slowly springs back. If the dough springs back quickly, it needs more time to rise.

Meanwhile, make the jam for the filling. Combine the strawberries, honey and lemon juice in a small saucepan. Cook over a low heat for around 7–10 minutes, stirring often and mashing the strawberries with the back of your spoon or a potato masher. The jam is ready when it has turned a deep red colour and is glossy and thick. Let cool completely.

Now to shape, bake and fill.

Recipe continues overleaf.

Flour a clean work surface and scrape the dough out onto it, dusting the top with some more flour. Roll the dough into a log and divide into 8 equal pieces.

With flour-dusted hands, shape each piece of dough into a ball and place on a lightly greased baking tray. Rub a little oil over each bun and cover the tray with a damp, clean tea (dish) towel, or place inside a clean bin bag and set aside somewhere warm for 20–30 minutes to rise until puffy; you can use the poke test again to tell if they're ready.

Meanwhile, preheat the oven to 200°C (180°C fan/400°F/gas 6).

Uncover the dough and bake for 8–12 minutes, rotating the tray halfway through, until golden brown. Remove from the oven and wrap the hot doughnuts in a clean tea towel for 5 minutes – this helps soften their crusts.

Brush the warm doughnuts with melted butter. Pour the sugar into a wide bowl and roll the buttered doughnuts in the sugar.

Cut a slit in the side of each doughnut and spoon in some cooled jam. Alternatively, add the jam to a piping/pastry bag or a sandwich bag with the corner snipped off. Poke a hole into each doughnut with the handle of a wooden spoon then pipe in the jam. Serve immediately – the doughnuts are best eaten the day they're made!

NOTES

You can use frozen strawberries, but there's no need to chop them up as they'll break down very easily as you cook them.

The instant mashed potato flakes help to hold more moisture in the dough, making the softest, squishiest doughnuts without needing to fry them.

If you don't have a stand mixer, you can use the 'slap and fold' method to knead the dough. After mixing the dough ingredients together and letting the rough dough sit for 15 minutes, tip the dough out onto a clean work surface. Lift it up and slap it down on the work surface while still holding onto the edge of it. Fold the dough over itself and repeat. Don't add any flour when you're doing this or the doughnuts will end up heavy. For more guidance, look up YouTube videos on the slap and fold dough kneading technique.

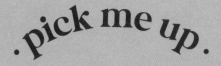

. pick me up .

Crispy Apple Nachos Platter

SERVES 4 · TAKES 45 MINUTES

The humble apple can be sliced, stewed, juiced, puréed, pickled and – a personal favourite – baked! This deliciously simple platter is a great way to hit that sweet spot and avoid wasting any apples facing fruit-bowl abandonment.

4 dessert apples, such as Gala or Jazz
8 tbsp low-fat plain yogurt
1 carrot, grated
80g (2¾oz) mixed nuts and seeds
Seeds of 1 pomegranate
8–10 mint leaves, finely sliced
2 tsp honey

Preheat your oven to 160°C (140°C fan/325°F/gas 3).

Core the apples and thinly slice them with their skins on. If you slice across the core and create circular apple discs, they will best hold their shape *and* they will look pretty. Arrange the slices on a baking tray lined with baking paper and bake for 40 minutes. Remove and leave to cool until crisp.

To serve, take a handful of apple crisps and pop them on a platter. Dollop on some yogurt, sprinkle with a little grated carrot, scatter with some nuts, seeds and mint, then drizzle with a little honey. Add another layer of apple crisps and repeat the toppings, then dive in.

NOTES

Store un-topped baked apple chips in an airtight container at room temperature for up to 1 week. You can also freeze them. Pop them into an airtight bag, squeezing as much air out as possible to avoid unwanted moisture. You can then eat these straight from the freezer or pop a handful in the oven and bake at to 160°C (140°C fan/325°F/ gas 3) for 15 minutes until thawed and dry.

If you don't want to bake your apples from scratch, you can buy dried apple slices from the supermarket and then top them following the recipe. You will need 500g (1lb 2oz) of store-bought dried apple slices.

Chickpea Cookie Dough

MAKES 480G (17OZ) DOUGH OR 22 SMALL COOKIES
TAKES 15 MINUTES

You don't visit Granny and Grandpa's without raiding the biscuit tin. Whether a Hobnob, a Lotus biscuit or a custard cream, a biscuit is always the perfect companion to a cuppa and a catch-up. But what beats a chocolate chip cookie? The cookie dough, of course! This sounds obscure, but I promise you'll achieve that same satisfying scoop of batter-like badness – but it's full of good things! Better yet, this cookie dough also makes actual baked cookies to dunk in your cuppa at the oldies.

1 x 400g (14oz) can of chickpeas
4 dates, pitted
60g (2¼oz) smooth almond butter
1 tsp vanilla bean paste
2 tbsp runny honey or dark brown sugar
Pinch of salt
100g (3½oz) dark (semisweet) chocolate
    chips (minimum 70% cocoa solids)

Tip the chickpeas and the liquid from their can into a small pan and add the pitted dates. Bring to a simmer over a medium–low heat and cook for 5 minutes to soften.

Drain the chickpeas and dates, reserving 60ml (2fl oz/¼ cup) of the cooking liquid, and add them to a food processor along with the almond butter, vanilla bean paste, honey (or sugar), salt and the reserved cooking liquid. Blitz until you have a really smooth dough – you'll need to pause and scrape the sides as you go, to make sure everything is incorporated.

Once smooth, fold in the chocolate chips and you're done! All you need now is a spoon and a little bit of self-restraint to not eat the whole lot!

WANT TO BAKE IT INTO COOKIES?

Simply add ½ teaspoon of bicarbonate of soda (baking soda) to the food processor with the other ingredients. Scoop heaped teaspoons of dough and drop onto a lined baking tray with a reasonable gap between each one. Flatten slightly (wet your fingertips to prevent sticking) and bake in an oven preheated to 200°C (180°C fan/400°F/gas 6) for 7–10 minutes. Leave to cool and firm up for 15 minutes before tucking in.

NOTES

Store the dough (uncooked) in the fridge in an airtight container for up to 3 days, or freeze in an airtight container for up to 3 months, and allow to thaw in the fridge for a minimum of 12 hours before eating.

If wanting to freeze the dough to make cookies, and you have added the bicarb, roll into cookie dough balls and freeze them, then simply bake from frozen for 8–10 minutes using the oven temperatures above.

JUST DESSERTS

Grilled Peaches with a Nutty Crumble

SERVES 4 · TAKES 25 MINUTES

Crumble is my favourite comfort dessert. Hunks of knobbly crumble turning to dough as they sink into the fruity filling. Not forgetting the COLD custard. Yes, cold. I can hear the audible gasp from a few of you but I promise you hot crumble with the cold custard is what dreams are made of.

60g (2¼oz) hazelnuts

40g (1½oz) pumpkin seeds

1 tsp ground cinnamon

¼ tsp ground ginger

Zest of 1 orange

2 tbsp maple syrup

2 tbsp coconut oil, melted

Pinch of salt

80g (2¾oz) rolled (porridge) oats

4 ripe peaches

Preheat the oven to 200°C (180°C fan/400°F/gas 6).

To a blender add your hazelnuts, pumpkin seeds, cinnamon, ginger, orange zest, maple syrup, 1 tablespoon of the melted coconut oil and the salt. Give it a couple of pulses to combine and chop the nuts into smaller chunks. Mix in the oats and then spread the crumble mixture out onto a baking tray. Bake for 10–12 minutes, giving it a little shimmy halfway through to make sure everything is turning evenly golden.

Slice your ripe peaches in half and remove the stone (pit). Brush lightly with the remaining melted coconut oil and pop onto a hot griddle pan. Cook for 2–3 minutes on each side until griddle marks form. You can also cook these in a normal frying pan.

Time to assemble. Pop your peach halves on a plate with a generous serving of crumble. Finish with a scoop of homemade 'ice cream' (page 208), a dollop of cold custard, a slick of cream or lashings of yogurt. Whatever tickles your fancy!

NOTES

Your nutty crumble can also make a delicious granola. Simply add a few handfuls of dried fruit and serve it with plain yogurt for an easy breakfast. Store the crumble in an airtight container at room temperature for up to 2 weeks, or in a sealed freezer bag in the freezer for up to 3 months.

Baked Vanilla Cheesecake

SERVES 4 · TAKES 1 HOUR 30 MINUTES

When I started driving when I was a teenager, I joined the growing convoy of cars that would drive to our local supermarket every lunchtime. On a Monday, I would purchase a New York vanilla cheesecake with a naive hope that I'd make it last to Friday, before proceeding to eat most of it.

FOR THE BISCUIT CRUMBLE
6 Rich Tea biscuits (cookies)
2 tbsp smooth almond butter
1 free-range egg white
3½ tbsp rolled (porridge) oats
Butter or margarine, softened, for greasing

FOR THE FILLING
1 free-range egg, separated
100g (3½oz) 0% fat Greek yogurt
100g (3½oz) low-fat cream cheese
½ tsp cornflour (cornstarch)
Juice of ½ lemon
2 tsp vanilla bean paste
30g (1oz) caster (superfine) sugar

NOTES

These can store once cooked in the fridge for up to 3 days, but they will deflate and are better made and eaten, or stored uncooked until you're ready. Refrigerate for as long as 24 hours before cooking from cold at 200°C (180°C fan/400°F/gas 6) for 40–45 minutes. Alternatively, you can freeze them uncooked for up to 7 days and then cook from frozen for 55 minutes.

Preheat the oven to 200°C (180°C fan/400°F/gas 6).

First make the biscuit crumble. Pop your Rich Tea biscuits in a bag and smash them to pieces with a rolling pin.

Mix the almond butter and egg white together in a small bowl, then tip in the biscuit crumbs and oats and stir to coat. Crumble onto a baking tray, spread out into an even layer and bake for 10–12 minutes until darkened and smelling toasty, then remove from the oven and set aside.

Turn the oven down to 180°C (160°C fan/350°F/gas 4).

Now make the filling. Whisk together the egg yolk, yogurt, cream cheese, cornflour, lemon juice and vanilla in a medium bowl until smooth.

In a separate bowl, whisk the egg white and sugar until white, thick and fluffy.

Gently fold the egg white into your yogurt mixture until fully combined, trying to keep as much air within the mixture as possible.

Grease four 125ml (4fl oz) ramekins with a light brush of softened butter or margarine and evenly decant your filling mixture into them.

We're going to cook this using a water bath. Grab a roasting dish, place your ramekins inside the dish and pour boiling water into the dish to come halfway up the sides of the ramekins.

Pop it all in the oven for 25–30 minutes until just about set but still wobbly in the middle when you give one a gentle shake. Remove from the water bath and let cool to room temperature before chilling in the fridge for at least 30 minutes.

Sprinkle on the crumble, grab a spoon and dive in.

JUST DESSERTS

Whipped Tofu Tiramisu

SERVES 4 · TAKES 2+ HOURS

My mother-in-law makes the best tiramisu. She is Italian, after all. Strong coffee, balanced with a rich vanilla cream and, uncompromisingly, lady fingers. I'm all for finding alternatives to make our favourite treats a little more 'good for us' but, in my book, a classic lady finger is essential to a tiramisu.

175ml (6fl oz/¾ cup) hot water
2 tbsp instant coffee granules
175g (6oz) silken tofu, drained
100g (3½oz) mascarpone
2 tbsp maple syrup
2 medium free-range egg whites
Small pinch of salt
100g (3½oz) lady/sponge fingers (savoiardi biscuits)
1 tbsp unsweetened cocoa powder

In a wide, shallow dish, combine the hot water and instant coffee granules, stirring to dissolve. Set aside to cool.

To a blender add the silken tofu, mascarpone, maple syrup and 2 tablespoons of the strong coffee. Blend until smooth and creamy, then pour into a bowl and set aside.

In a separate, medium bowl, whisk the egg whites with the salt until you get firm peaks. Take a heaped spoonful of the egg whites and stir into the mascarpone mixture to loosen. Add the remaining egg whites and fold together gently until the egg whites have been fully incorporated.

Dip each of your lady fingers into the cooled coffee, giving them a chance to soak up the coffee but not turn too soggy. Layer these into a serving dish until you've used half the lady fingers, then spread over half of the creamy filling. Repeat once more to use up the remaining lady fingers and creamy filling. Dust with a generous layer of cocoa powder (this is key to a great tiramisu!) then cover and chill for at least a few hours before serving.

NOTES

If you don't like the idea of raw egg whites, you can substitute 100ml (3½fl oz/scant ½ cup) aquafaba (the liquid from a can of chickpeas), whipped with ¼ teaspoon of lemon juice or vinegar until you get firm peaks. Aquafaba takes longer to whip than egg whites so just stick with it for a few minutes to get the right consistency.

This will store happily in the fridge for up to 2 days. It also freezes really well! Wrap the dish lightly in a double layer of cling film (plastic wrap) and a layer of foil and freeze for up to 3 months. Thaw the tiramisu in the fridge overnight and eat within 2 days.

Sticky Vanilla and Treacle Toffee Pudding

SERVES 4 · TAKES 1 HOUR

My brother adopted the same sweet tooth as my mum and dad (I'm the savoury-craving anomaly) so it's no surprise that sticky toffee pudding is his favourite dessert. That honey-caramel sweetness engulfing a light sponge is unbeatable...

.

75g (2½oz) pitted dates
80g (2¾oz) just-boiled water
1½ tbsp olive or vegetable oil
1 medium free-range egg
1 tsp black treacle
1 tsp vanilla bean paste
75g (2½oz) rolled (porridge) oats
½ tsp baking powder
¼ tsp bicarbonate of soda (baking soda)
Reduced-fat crème fraîche, to serve

FOR THE SAUCE
50g (1¾oz) unsalted butter
6 tbsp maple syrup
2 tsp black treacle
60g (2¼oz) low-fat cream cheese
2 tsp vanilla bean paste

Preheat the oven to 180°C (160°C fan/350°F/gas 4) and line a 450g (1lb) loaf pan with baking paper.

Begin by soaking the pitted dates in the boiling water for 15 minutes to soften. Tip the soaked dates and water into a blender along with the oil, egg, treacle and vanilla. Blend until smooth, then add the oats, baking powder and bicarbonate of soda and blend again to get a pourable batter. (If you want a fine-textured sponge, you can blitz the oats in the blender too.)

Pour the batter into your lined loaf pan and bake for 30–35 minutes until the cake springs back when poked and a skewer inserted into its centre comes out clean.

Meanwhile, for the sauce, heat the butter, maple syrup and treacle in a small saucepan set over a low heat until melted together and starting to bubble. Add the cream cheese and stir vigorously (I like to use a small whisk) until you have a smooth sauce.

Remove from the heat and mix in the vanilla, then pour the sauce all over the top of your cooked sticky toffee pudding or decant into a jug (pitcher) and let your diners slather it on themselves. Serve each slice with a dollop of crème fraîche.

NOTES

Store any leftovers in the fridge for up to 5 days. The sponge can be reheated on low power in a microwave for 1–2 minutes.

You can also just knock up this sauce for ice cream or to drizzle over your pancakes and French toast!

JUST DESSERTS

Gooey Chocolate Cake with a Thick, Fluffy Frosting

SERVES 10 · TAKES 1 HOUR 30 MINUTES

I was a bookworm growing up and the magical fantasies of Roald Dahl captivated me, even his most revolting foods. But no one can deny the glossy and gorgeous ribbons of thick chocolate cream, sandwiched between moist, springy chocolate sponges that make chocolate cake the most scrumptious cake in the entire world.

75ml (2½fl oz/5 tbsp) olive or vegetable oil, plus extra for greasing (or use softened butter)

150g (5½oz) carrots, finely grated

120g (4¼oz) runny honey or granulated sugar

80ml (2¾fl oz/5 tbsp) water

2 medium free-range eggs

2 tsp vanilla bean paste

180g (6¼oz) wholemeal (wholewheat) flour

30g (1oz) unsweetened cocoa powder, plus extra for dusting

1½ tsp baking powder

½ tsp bicarbonate of soda (baking soda)

FOR THE FROSTING

2 ripe avocados, peeled, halved and pitted

80g (2¾oz) runny honey

40g (1½oz) unsweetened cocoa powder

100g (3½oz) dark chocolate, melted

1 tsp vanilla bean paste

Pinch of salt

Preheat the oven to 210°C (190°C fan/410°F/gas 6–7). Grease two 18cm (7in) round cake pans with a little oil or softened butter and line the bases with baking paper.

In a medium bowl, stir together the oil, grated carrots, honey (or sugar), water, eggs and vanilla until combined.

Fold in the flour, cocoa powder, baking powder and bicarbonate of soda until just combined and no floury patches remain.

Divide the mixture between the prepared cake pans and bake for 20–25 minutes until a skewer poked into the centre of the cake comes out clean. Allow to cool at room temperature for 10 minutes before tipping out onto a wire rack and leaving to cool completely.

Add all the ingredients for the frosting to a blender or food processor and whizz until super-smooth. Slather half the smooth chocolate cream onto one of the cooled sponges. Sandwich with the other sponge and then top it all off with the remaining chocolate cream. Dust with a little more chocolate powder, then slice it up and serve!

NOTES

If you like things a little sweeter, make the strawberry jam (jelly) from page 193 and spoon a little of that between the sponges too.

Caramelized Banana Split with a Cherry on Top

SERVES 4 · TAKES 1 HOUR

'You can't eat all that?!' A wildly incorrect assumption from my parents as I order the sharing split all to myself. I'm often referred to as the 'bottomless pit' because I have an endless capacity to eat, but when food is this good... how do you stop?

FOR THE STRAWBERRY 'ICE CREAM'
300g (10½oz) frozen strawberries
200g (7oz) 0% fat Greek yogurt
1 tbsp balsamic vinegar
1 tbsp honey (if it needs sweetening)

FOR THE VANILLA AND BANANA 'ICE CREAM'
250g (9oz) 0% fat Greek yogurt
300g (10½oz) frozen bananas, peeled and sliced
1 tbsp maple syrup
1 tsp vanilla bean paste

FOR THE CHOCOLATE 'ICE CREAM'
200g (7oz) 0% fat Greek yogurt
60g (2¼oz) dark (semisweet) chocolate
 (minimum 70% cocoa solids), melted
300g (10½oz) frozen bananas, peeled and sliced
2 tbsp maple syrup
1 tbsp unsweetened cocoa powder

FOR THE BANANAS
60g (2¼oz) walnuts
2 tsp brown sugar
1 tsp ground cinnamon
4 bananas

FOR THE CREAM (MAKES ENOUGH
FOR 4 BANANA SPLITS)
60ml (2fl oz/¼ cup) whipping (heavy) cream
120g (4¼oz) 0% fat Greek yogurt
1 tsp runny honey

FOR THE SAUCE
1 tsp cornflour (cornstarch)
6 tbsp water
160g (5¾oz) frozen pitted cherries
Juice of ½ lemon

For the strawberry 'ice cream', chuck your ingredients into a blender or food processor and blitz for 1–2 minutes, stopping to scrape down the sides, until smooth and creamy. Decant into a freezer container and freeze until needed. Repeat in a clean blender for the vanilla and banana ice cream.

To make the chocolate ice cream, add the yogurt to a clean blender or food processor and start whizzing while adding the melted chocolate. Add the frozen bananas, maple syrup and cocoa powder and blitz again, stopping to scrape down the sides as needed, until smooth and creamy. Decant into a freezer container and freeze until needed.

For the bananas, blitz or bash up your walnuts into a fine crumb and combine with your sugar and cinnamon in a wide shallow dish. Slice each of your bananas in half lengthways, then gently press them into the walnut crumb. Cook the coated bananas in a lightly greased pan set over a medium–low heat for 4–6 minutes until golden on each side.

For the cream, ensure your ingredients are straight out the fridge to get the best 'whip' possible. Simply whip your whipping cream into soft peaks with an electric whisk (or hand whisk if you have uninhibited enthusiasm), then whisk in the yogurt and honey until you have stiff peaks.

Finally make the sauce. Add the cornflour and 1 tablespoon of the water to a small pan, stirring to get a thin paste. Add the cherries, the remaining water and the lemon juice. Bring to the boil over a medium–low heat, then reduce to a simmer and cook until thickened and glossy. Allow to cool a little.

To assemble the banana splits, place one scoop of each ice cream in a bowl with a cooked banana half on each side of the scoops. Top each scoop with some of the whipped cream and finally spoon over some of the cherries and their juice.

JUST DESSERTS

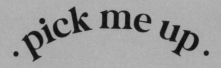

Club Tropicana Fro-Yo

SERVES 4 · TAKES 5 MINUTES

'Ice Cream' became its own food group on our holidays to Majorca. It seemed impossible to end a meal without visiting the local gelato shop, so when we got home Mum and Dad had to keep our cravings satisfied while trying to ensure things were remotely healthy – and this is the genius way to do it.

250g (9oz) frozen pineapple
5cm (2in) piece of frozen ginger
Juice of 1 clementine
200g (7oz) 0% fat Greek yogurt
1 tbsp honey (if it needs sweetening)

Chuck your ingredients into a blender or food processor and blitz for 1–2 minutes, stopping to scrape down the sides, until smooth and creamy. Eat immediately or decant into a freezer container and freeze until needed.

Lemon Curd
Meringue Pies

MAKES 6 · TAKES 35 MINUTES

I used to live next door to Evanthia, a beautiful Greek grandma who force-fed us at every opportunity and has a garden overflowing with beautiful climbing flowers and plants. I've taken clippings from all her best bloomers – the fig tree, the plum tree, the spider plants, and the aloe vera. The next on my list is her incredible lemon tree.

FOR LAYER 1: THE TART CASE
3 sheets of filo (phyllo) pastry
Low-calorie butter spray

FOR LAYER 2: THE LEMON CURD
Zest and juice of 2 large lemons
80g (2¾oz) honey
2 large free-range eggs
15g (½oz) butter

FOR LAYER 3: THE MERINGUE
1 free-range egg white
2 tbsp caster (superfine) sugar
¼ tsp lemon juice

NOTES

Use the leftover egg yolk in my creamy masala scrambled eggs (page 10) to make them extra rich!

Preheat the oven to 220°C (200°C fan/425°F/gas 7).

Cut each sheet of filo pastry into 4 (so you have 12 squares).

Spray 6 holes of a muffin tray each with 1 pump of low-calorie butter spray. Push a filo square into each hole, shaping it into the edges (try using the base of a cup/glass that's smaller than the muffin hole to help shape it). Spray each filo case with a few pumps of butter spray, lay on another square of filo, then spray a few times again.

Pop your filo cases into the oven and bake for 8–12 minutes until the edges of your pastry cases are golden-brown. Set aside to cool and crisp up.

Place the lemon zest and juice in a medium, heatproof bowl along with the honey and eggs and whisk together until smooth. Place over a pan of gently simmering water (a bain marie – see page 13) and stir often until the mixture thickens. Once thickened, remove from the heat and stir in the butter, then leave to cool to room temperature. Chill until needed. (If you prefer a sweeter lemon curd, then sneak in some extra honey.)

To make the meringue, whisk the egg white, sugar and lemon juice (the lemon helps stabilize the meringue) in a small, heatproof bowl set over a small pan of simmering water (in the same manner you cooked the curd) until you get stiff peaks. (I recommend using an electric whisk so your arm doesn't fall off!) Remove from the heat.

Fill each cooled filo case with 2 tablespoons of the lemon curd, then pipe or spoon on the meringue mixture. If you have a blowtorch, give each meringue a blast so the edges turn golden. Otherwise, you can achieve a similar effect by quickly placing them under a hot, preheated oven grill (broiler) – be careful not to place them too close to the grill and keep an eye on them to avoid any burnt meringue or pastry!

JUST DESSERTS

Not-So-Classic Trifle

MAKES 6 INDIVIDUAL TRIFLES · TAKES 1 HOUR 45 MINUTES

You know that cupboard full of small glass ramekins from the dine-in meal you had four Valentine's days ago, or that random time you splashed out on a posh yogurt, because you needed a little lift...? Their time has finally come! Alternatively, grab whatever glasses you have in the cupboard.

FOR LAYER 1: THE SPONGE
Butter, for greasing
4 large free-range eggs
100g (3½oz) caster (superfine) sugar
130g (4¾oz) wholemeal (wholewheat) flour
2 tsp baking powder

FOR LAYER 2: THE JELLY
1 x 135g (4¾oz) packet of sugar-free
    raspberry jelly (jello) cubes
150ml (5fl oz/scant ⅔ cup) boiling water
150ml (5fl oz/scant ⅔ cup) cold water
120g (4¼oz) raspberries

FOR LAYER 3: THE CUSTARD
275ml (9½fl oz/scant 1¼ cups) skimmed milk
1 tbsp plus 2 tsp cornflour (cornstarch)
2 tbsp runny honey (or granulated sugar)
2 medium free-range egg yolks
1 tsp vanilla bean paste
Pinch of salt

FOR LAYER 4: THE CREAM
80g (2¾oz) whipping (heavy) cream
100g (3½oz) 0% fat Greek yogurt

NOTES

This dish can also be made in one large dish rather than as individual trifles. You can cook the cake in a 20cm (8in) round cake pan, baking it at the same temperature for 15–20 minutes, for a thicker sponge that can be chopped into fingers to line a large trifle dish.

Preheat the oven to 200°C (180°C fan/400°F/gas 6). Grease and line a 26 x 19.5cm (10¼ x 7¾in) Swiss roll tin. Have ready 6 ramekins (I usually use 200ml/7fl oz ones, each about 10cm/4in high) or small glasses.

For the sponge, beat the eggs and sugar together until thickened and fluffy. Fold in the flour and baking powder, decant into the prepared tin and bake in the oven for 8–10 minutes or until a skewer inserted in the middle comes out clean. Due to how thinly the batter is spread, this will make a flat but light sponge, perfect for the base of an individual serving.

Once your thin sponge has cooled, use a cookie cutter slightly smaller than your ramekins to cut out discs. Pop a disc in the bottom of each ramekin. You can eat the cake scraps if you want, or freeze them in an airtight container for up to 3 months – they can be used to make the delicious raspberry and almond cake truffles on page 216.

Separate the raspberry jelly into cubes and place in a heatproof bowl. Add the boiling water and stir until dissolved. Add the cold water and stir (this will make the jelly double strength). Pour over the sponges and add your raspberries. Pop them in the fridge to set.

Make the custard. Warm the milk in a small pan over a medium heat until gently steaming. Mix the cornflour, honey, egg yolks, vanilla and salt in a bowl, then slowly whisk in the warmed milk. Pour the mixture back into the pan and stir over a low–medium heat, bringing the custard to a gentle boil to thicken your custard and cook out the cornflour – removing any floury taste and texture. Remove from the heat and allow to cool to room temperature.

Once the jelly has set, pour your custard over the top and return the trifles to the fridge while you prepare your final layer.

Ensure your ingredients for the cream are straight out the fridge to get the best 'whip' possible. Simply whip the cream into soft peaks with an electric whisk (or hand whisk if you have uninhibited enthusiasm), then stir in the yogurt until combined. Use this to top each of the trifles, then serve.

Raspberry and Almond Cake Truffles

MAKES 10 · TAKES 45 MINUTES

It's tradition to eat cake on your birthday, so a mouthful of light sponge, smothered in buttercream in varying tantalizing flavours, always brings a feeling of celebration. Celebrate the everyday with these little nuggets!

FOR THE TRUFFLES

100g (3½oz) leftover sponge cake (from the trifle on page 215)
2 tbsp ground almonds
1 tbsp poppy seeds
Zest of 1 lemon
90g (3¼oz) low-fat cream cheese
1 tbsp smooth almond butter
1 tbsp runny honey
60g (2¼oz) frozen raspberries, crumbled

FOR THE COATING

60g (2¼oz) smooth almond butter
25g (1oz) coconut oil
1 tsp runny honey
1 tbsp sprinkles or crumbled freeze-dried raspberries, to decorate

Crumble the sponge cake into a medium bowl. Mix in the ground almonds, poppy seeds and lemon zest. Make a well in the centre of the mixture and add the cream cheese, almond butter and honey. Stir to get a soft mixture that holds together when pressed into a ball. Sprinkle in the frozen raspberries and gently mix to distribute evenly.

Scoop out heaped tablespoons of the mixture and roll into balls. Set on a plate in the freezer to chill for 20 minutes so they firm up and get cold.

About 10 minutes before you're ready to coat the truffles, warm the almond butter, coconut oil and honey in a small pan over a low heat, stirring constantly just until the coconut oil melts.

Remove from the heat and set aside to cool so it can thicken up a bit but is still fluid. Dip each cake truffle into the coating and set onto a lined baking tray, then sprinkle the top with a pinch of sprinkles or freeze-dried raspberries. Chill until set – around 15 minutes – before eating.

NOTES

Store the truffles in an airtight container in the fridge for up to 3 days, or freeze for up to 3 months, allowing them to thaw in the fridge overnight before consuming.

JUST DESSERTS

Sticky Pineapple Upside Down Cake

SERVES 6–8 · TAKES 45 MINUTES

Whether cutting it up and sticking it on a cocktail stick with a cube of cheap Cheddar at a birthday party, or cracking open a can when I get home from school, there's something about that perfectly sweet, canned pineapple that fills me with joy and childlike comfort.

Butter or oil, for greasing

2 tbsp light brown sugar

1 x 435g (15oz) can of pineapple rings in natural juice

3 medium free-range eggs

65g (2¼oz) caster (superfine) sugar

50g (1¾oz) wholemeal (wholewheat) flour

½ tsp baking powder

20g (¾oz) cornflour (cornstarch)

40g (1½oz) unsweetened desiccated (dried shredded) coconut, plus an extra 2 tbsp to decorate (see Note)

1 red chilli, deseeded and finely chopped

Preheat the oven to 200°C (180°C fan/400°F/gas 6). Grease a 23cm (9in) springform cake pan and line with baking paper, then sprinkle over the light brown sugar.

Open the can of pineapple rings (oh, the joy). Place a single layer of rings in the bottom of your cake pan. The chef's treat is to munch on any remaining pineapple rings as you make the cake, but please set aside the juice!

Beat together the eggs and caster sugar in a medium bowl with an electric whisk until thick, fluffy and pale, around 2–3 minutes. Fold in the flour, baking powder, cornflour and desiccated coconut. Once combined, pour into your cake pan, covering the pineapple.

Bake in the oven for 15–20 minutes until a skewer inserted into the centre comes out clean. Remove from the oven and allow to stand for 5–10 minutes before turning out onto a serving plate.

Meanwhile, toast the 2 tablespoons of desiccated coconut in a small frying pan over a medium heat, stirring constantly until it starts to turn golden – watch it carefully as it can burn easily. Remove from the heat and tip onto a plate so it stops cooking.

Simmer the juice from the pineapple can in a small saucepan until reduced by about half. Pour this syrup over the cake and top with some chopped chilli (strange but delicious) and a sprinkle of the toasted coconut. Let it cool completely before slicing.

NOTE

If you're not a fan of coconut, you can swap the desiccated coconut in the batter for ground almonds. Top with 2 tablespoons of toasted flaked (slivered) almonds instead.

Index

quinoa stuffing, roasted squash with 177

ramen, veg-packed silky tofu 156
raspberry and almond cake truffles 216
raspberry jelly (jello): not-so-classic trifle 215
rendang: beef rendang kebabs 160
rice: squid and samphire risotto 129
  Thai green curry fried rice 148
Rich Tea biscuits (cookies): baked vanilla cheesecake 200
ricotta: fig and ricotta pizza 142
  gooey summer berry and ricotta stuffed French toast 18
  lasagne with a ricotta bechamel and pork ragu 48
risotto, squid and samphire 129

salads: bang bang slaw 38
  courgette salad 142
  grilled mango and prawn noodle salad 112
  pickled slaw tabbouleh 84
  purple potato salad 80
  quick pickled salad 155
  saucy Caesar salad cups 76
  sticky roasted parsnip and apple salad 172
  super green salad 83
  tuna pesto picnic pasta salad 111
salmon: lime-infused salmon skewers 116
  see also smoked salmon
salsa verde, pea and avocado 85
salsas: avocado and citrus salsa 85
  corn salsa 119
samphire: squid and samphire risotto 129
sandwiches: fish fingers in mushy pea baps 107
sausages: skinless pork and apple sausages, creamy mash and mushroom gravy 52
Scotch egg, baked breakfast 14
seeded soda bread cheese toastie 34
shallots, slow-roasted red cabbage and 173
skewers: beef rendang kebabs 160
  lime-infused salmon skewers 116
slaw: bang bang slaw 38
  pickled slaw tabbouleh 84
smoked haddock: lentil and smoked haddock kedgeree 104
smoked salmon: avocado and crushed pea with salmon 26
  lemony smoked salmon mousse 127
soups: chunky minestrone soup 89–90
  leek, pea and potato soup 87
  roasted tomato and garlic soup 92

spinach: poached eggs with cheat's hollandaise and spinach 13
  secret spinach Scotch pancakes 21
  spinach and parsley pikelets 130
  spinach pasta 59–60
squash: roasted squash with quinoa stuffing 177
squid and samphire risotto 129
stew, beef 67
sticky vanilla and treacle toffee pudding 204
strawberries: caramelized banana split 208
strawberry jam (jelly): baked strawberry doughnuts 193–4
stroganoff, beef and mushroom 59–60
sweet potatoes: gnocchi dumplings 67
  sweet potato hash sunny side up 72
sweetcorn: corn salsa 119

tabbouleh, pickled slaw 84
tacos, mackerel fish 119
tahini flapjack, date caramel and dark chocolate millionaires 190
tartare sauce 107
Thai green corn cobs 75
Thai green curry fried rice 148
Thai-style fish cakes 115
tiramisu, whipped tofu 203
toastie, seeded soda bread cheese 34
toffee: sticky vanilla and treacle toffee pudding 204
tofu: crunchy tofu croutons 76
  veg-packed silky tofu ramen 156
  whipped tofu tiramisu 203
tomatoes: pizza 141, 143
  poached eggs in a spicy tomato and bean sauce 22
  roasted tomato and garlic soup 92
  tomato ketchup 16
tortilla chip nachos with chilli 134
tortilla pizzas 3 ways 143
traybake, spiced chicken and loaded veggie 68
trifle, not-so-classic 215
tuna: tuna and onion pizza 142
  tuna pesto picnic pasta salad 111
turkey: charred chilli pepper con carne 56–8
tzatziki, zingy 96

vegetables: cheesy root veg fries 152
  green vegetable pasta bake 99
  simple scrap crisps 181
  spiced chicken and loaded veggie traybake 68
  veg-packed silky tofu ramen 156
  veggie-stuffed Yorkshire pudding pies 183

veggie loaf: moreish mushroom and walnut loaf 174

waffles, cheesy cauliflower 31
walnuts: moreish mushroom and walnut loaf 174

yogurt: caramelized banana split 208
  Club Tropicana fro-yo 211
  mustard 'mayo' 16
  tartare sauce 107
  zingy tzatziki 96
Yorkshire pudding pies, veggie-stuffed 183

THANK YOU

Thank you

My kitchen inspiration – Mum and Dad at catering school in 1980.

At the risk of this sounding like an Oscar acceptance speech, I need to establish that my gratitude is not only to the people who helped bring this book together, but to those whose impact on my life has brought me to this very surreal moment.

I often state, I was 'born lucky'. That is mainly due to being born to my parents, Brian and Jo. Born to the two most loving, supportive, inspiring and motivating humans. Born into a family whose motto was 'you can do anything', and who did anything to protect and enable that belief. From scoffing everyday meals, to indulging in every memorable get-together you created for everyone around you, it was inevitable that I would follow you both into a career in food. *Everyday Comfort* celebrates the meals that give us that warm fuzzy feeling. That, for me, is any dish eaten with you.

To my husband, Simon. This book would not exist without your support, your patience and your palate. You are the most impressive human I have ever met, and Katie Pix couldn't have survived, let alone thrived, were you not the foundation of our family. This book is for you and for the lifetime of dream-come-true adventures we have to come.

To my family. All of my grandparents whose dinner tables cemented my most treasured memories. My brother, who has sacrificed many second helpings to my 'food panic' over the years and makes me a very proud little sister. To the family I've gained, whose Italian and South African roots have enriched my life with amazing food, unforgettable moments and unrepeatable phrases. To my aunts, uncles and cousins, who baked with me, ate with me and turned the dinner table into a theatrical spectacle – complete with uncles dressed in mankinis – you made me never want to grow up.

To my friends. My childhood friends, my school friends, my uni friends, my work friends, my Essex-Roaders, my friends I've stolen from Si – my people.

It's a cliché but friends really are your chosen family, and I am so grateful for your unwavering support and the ease and joy of your company.

To my G. A special mention for the work-wife. This freelance life can be a lonely business, but you have been my soundboard, my confidante and my biggest cheerleader. It seemed highly unnecessary that I'd need any more wonderful humans in my life and then you rocked up and have become such a fundamental part of me. Can't wait to see you take over the world.

To my opportunity makers. Now we're really going back, but part of my belief in being 'born lucky' is that my path through life has led me time and time again to brilliant people. My first proper bosses, Mark Maddox and Steve Berry, who introduced me to the (then) burgeoning world of social media. Jamie Oliver and Richard Herd, who humoured my ambitions to be in front of the camera and rallied the troops to make it happen. Dom Smales and Lucy Loveridge, who fancied taking a total punt on me and laid the path for this wild and wonderful journey. To every person who has looped me into an email, vouched for me, vetted stuff for me, picked up a camera to help me – thank you.

To my teammates. Harriet, queen of publishing – I'm not sure I will ever stop questioning how lucky I am that you scrolled across me and saw something. With Emily and the team at Quadrille, we have created something I am so proud of. Thank you for giving me a treasure I can share with my future grandchildren. Pip, what a full-circle moment. Since meeting you at Jamie's, I never dreamed there would be a day that your incredible talent would be used to style my book. Sarah, you were magic throughout the process too! Libby, I can't thank you enough for bringing my recipes to life with all the stunning props. Izy, we did it! I hoped one day I would be asking you to capture my first cookbook, and it's bigger and better than my wildest dreams. You are the very best at what you do, and I am so grateful to have been welcomed into your home as well as your studio. Cheers to many more pints with Andy!

To my community. Those who started following from YouTube, bore with me when I tried to hop on all the trends during the dreary days of Covid and continued to indulge in my food and antics across the world wide web. This is all because of you. This is nothing short of extraordinary. With my whole heart, thank you.

Managing Director
Sarah Lavelle

**Commissioning
and Project Editor**
Harriet Webster

Copy Editor
Sally Somers

Art Direction and Design
Emily Lapworth

Illustration
Katie Pix

Photographer
Izy Hossack

Food Stylist
Pip Spence

Assistant Food Stylist
Sarah Vassallo

Prop Stylist
Libby Silberman

Make-up Artist
Becky Pursey & Bobbi Brown

Hair Stylist
Adam Cooke

Nail Technician
Emily Hasler,
Bee Beauty By Emily

Head of Production
Stephen Lang

Senior Production Controller
Gary Hayes

First published in 2024 by
Quadrille Publishing Limited

Quadrille
52–54 Southwark Street
London SE1 1UN
quadrille.com

Text © Katie Pix 2024
Photography © Izy Hossack 2024
Design and layout © Quadrille 2024

Cataloguing in Publication Data: a catalogue record
for this book is available from the British Library.

ISBN: 978 1 83783 118 0

Printed in China

Many thanks to **John Lewis** and **Waitrose**,
who kindly donated clothing and props, and to
Carrie Elizabeth, who kindly gifted jewellery,
for the photoshoot.

Find more recipes from Katie on **Instagram** and
TikTok (@thekatiepix), **YouTube** (@katiepix) or
on her **website** (katiepix.com).